Gone Fishin'...

The **75**

Best Waters
in
Connecticut

Gone Fishin'...

The 75

Best Waters in Connecticut

By Manny Luftglass

Gone Fishin' Enterprises
PO Box 556, Annandale, New Jersey 08801

Pictured on the cover: *(On the left.)* (I like his cap!) Jim DuBois caught this 6 lb. brown trout on a deep running crank bait across from the boat launch at East Twin Lake in the spring of 2000. *(In the middle.)* Dr. George Lowy hit this 8 lb. bonito at the Norwalk Islands on an 8 inch deceiver fly. *(On the right.)* Mace Vitale caught this big largemouth bass at Rodgers Lake.

Pictured on the back cover: Here's the author with a 10 lb. northern, just before releasing it.

Gone Fishin' ... The 75 Best Waters in Connecticut
By Manny Luftglass

© 2001 Emanuel Luftglass

Published By
Gone Fishin' Enterprises
PO Box 556, Annandale, New Jersey 08801

ISBN: 0-9650261-7-5
UPC: 7 9338097531-9

Photo Credits:
O'Hara's Landing, Capt. Jeff Northrop, Troy Klauder, my daughter Barb, Governor Rowland, The Fisheries Division of the Connecticut DEP, Capt. Sal Tardella, Tom Boyd, Capt. Joe Devine, Capt. David Orlowski, Capt. Bryan Hocking, Craig Mergens of Riverfront Recapture, Inc., Grady Allen, and Ron Whiteley, along with personal photos by the author.
Most of the fish pictured herein were released alive!
Map Credit: Published annually by AAA, Heathrow, FL 32746. 2001 Edition.

Design & Typography:
TeleSet
Hillsborough, New Jersey

PRINTED IN THE UNITED STATES OF AMERICA

Dedication

And why did I pick Connecticut
for my tenth "Gone Fishin' " book?
Simple! The waters of Connecticut
hold a wide variety of fish
and the people who are interested in the hobby here
are truly dedicated to their sport!

Whether we are talking about the countless anglers
who fish her waters,
the employees of the Department of Environmental
Protection's (DEP) Fisheries Division,
or the skippers who work hard to earn their living
bringing anglers to fish,
or folks who belong to great clubs like Trout Unlimited,
and certainly those who slave for hours on end
trying to accommodate anglers at their stores,
all of them deserve
a tip of my "Gone Fishin' " cap in thanks.

I dedicate this book to all of the above anglers,
and ask you to enjoy our hobby and above all else,
obey the law.

Contents

Foreword

By John G. Roland, Governor of Connecticut

My family and I have enjoyed many of Connecticut's fine natural resources from the hills to the shore. One activity that stands out above all the others is fishing. I grew up here and as a child spent summers fishing the waters of Bantam Lake for northern pike and catfish. Now as a parent, I take my children out on the water to enjoy the thrill of reeling in a big one.

Connecticut offers some of the finest fresh water fishing opportunities in the entire northeast. People travel from afar to fish for trout on the Farmington, Housatonic and Willimantic Rivers. Several regional and national tournaments have been held on the Connecticut River confirming our state's high standing among both amateur and professional anglers as they have competed side-by-side for a prized catch.

In addition to fresh water fishing, Connecticut offers exciting salt-water fishing opportunities. Whether you are striped bass fishing or angling for bluefish, fluke or scup, a day on Long Island Sound is a truly enjoyable experience. Connecticut's coastal waters have improved dramatically, and species such as weakfish present new and exciting opportunities the likes of which have not been seen for over 20 years!

Come to Connecticut to enjoy fishing and other wonderful attractions. Try a few spots and pick your own favorite, or choose one from this book. Either way, you will have a wonderful experience. And, please take a kid fishing with you — the memories will last a lifetime.

Sincerely,

JOHN G. ROWLAND
Governor

Connecticut Governor and Mrs. John G. Rowland.

Author's Preface

C onnecticut! I have fished her rivers, both brackish and fresh. Ditto some of its lakes, as well as the Sound.

But to make sure that I got it all right, I turned to many a local expert for help with in-depth details.

Within *"Gone Fishin' The 75 Best Waters in Connecticut,"* you will read about some saltwater hot spots from skippers of head boats and charter boats. Bait and Tackle stores from one end of the state to the other provided substantial help, and as you will read, "Redmoon" was one of my major contributors of quality data. Lots of people who work for Commissioner Arthur J. Rocque Jr., at the State DEP gave me material and without their assistance, this book would not have been possible.

My first contact was with DEP Natural Resources Bureau Chief Ed Parker who steered me to several members of his very fine staff. A few of those people include Supervising Fisheries Biologist Bill Hyatt, who, with help from other members of the Inland Fisheries Division biologists like Chuck Phillips and Jerry Leonard, put together what they consider "Top Spots For Fishing Connecticut" and I certainly included many of those waters herein.

Special thanks goes to Lori St. Amand for helping me coordinate the research with the DEP.

Stocking

Eileen B. O'Donnell, of DEP's Fisheries Division, sent me a wealth of material about the fish that her department stocks into the waters of Connecticut, and to her, I am deeply indebted. She also provided information regarding electrofishing surveys, etc., and from these documents, I was able to pick and choose data to provide to you regarding most of the freshwater sites written about in this book. Please note that some waters are added and others are deleted from time to time, so some details may not always be accurate.

Laws

Since laws change as often as seasons do, I may talk about some of them within the book, but please realize that they do change and in order to be truly up-to-date, you should read your copy of the Connecticut Anglers Guide that is given to you each year that you renew your license.

Special Regulations

Whenever we talk about a "Special Regulation" in this book, please realize that such regs do change from time to time so once again, make sure to read Guide!

Introduction

Why did my book about Pennsylvania only contain 50 locations? Simple, it has no saltwater of its own. And why did our New Jersey and New York books have 100 spots? Well, because they have an ocean too, not just a "Sound!"

We will start with Saltwater, covering the hot spots that exist in the Sound, but since most charter and head boats that sail from Connecticut ports cross over into the New York area of the Sound, we will talk about those slightly further areas to the south also. And of course, if we are discussing salt, we cannot exclude the waters off of Montauk since many Eastern Connecticut boats head out that way for cod, tuna, shark, etc. (So buy my New York book!)

I will show locations in alphabetical order per chapter in the table of contents, and where two different names may apply to a single site, the secondary name will cross reference to the primary name.

Next will come the rivers that flow into the Sound, with the alphabet again as my guide.

Following that will be moving bodies that are strictly freshwater, with the same order as just discussed.

And last will be the lakes and ponds that cover the state. Here again, we will travel around via the alphabet. Where a lake has two names, I will list it under its more commonly used name but in the table of contents, I will show where it can be found also with its alias.

In each grouping of locations, other than the various rivers, the map found in the book will have a corresponding number of the location to indicate the approximate place that it is found at. The saltwater sites will be just that — approximate! As to the rivers, since they cover so much area, consult with each site in the book to find where you might want to locate a section to fish in.

We will start the Lake/Reservoir chapter at Amos Lake and end with Lake Zoar but in order to keep things easy, any lake that starts with the word "Lake" will be placed in order of their proper name. So with Zoar, it will be under Z and not L, got it?

To repeat, you will find each of my sites on the imprint of the state contained herein, with its corresponding number as close to the exact waters as humanly possible. Hopefully, you will be able to find the spot that way, but since each lake, etc., is identified by the closest town, you should be able to locate it too with your own map or Atlas. I also used the copy of the Official Tourism Map that Connecticut puts out to help identify where the lakes are.

Please note that we will not discuss health advisories at all. The Summary gives you sufficient warnings and since the book's intent is to tell you where you can catch fish for fun and isn't intended to be a cook book, a word to the wise is sufficient, I hope.

CHAPTER 1

Saltwater

F irst, about the Sound itself. A newsletter copy from the DEP provided some useful information that I want to share with you. Interesting to note was that this estuary (an estuary is a body of water in which salt from the ocean mixes with fresh water from rivers and land) runs east and west. Most of them run north to south.

Long Island Sound has two openings where salt comes in and goes out. To the east, it runs through The Race and out to sea. The western opening goes through the East River and New York Harbor.

Fishermen from Westchester County and Long Island share the bounty of the Sound with their Connecticut neighbors. In fact, some of the head boats found in the Sound sail out of City Island in the Bronx.

The Sound is 21 miles across at its widest point and ranges approximately 110 miles long from east to west.

And where can you go and catch fish? Well, if you exit to the east, and many charter and party boats do just that, the ocean beckons with Montauk, one of the most famous words along the eastern seaboard, is right there. Montauk, with its cod, tuna, sharks, etc., is not much of a ride for the faster boats, especially those that sail from easterly sections of Connecticut's shore.

But when it comes to fishing in and around the Sound itself, let's pick some spots for you to visit, ones that expert anglers have told me about in detail. Starting in alphabetical order, followed by Buoy # 32A, here goes:

1 — BARTLETT REEF, WATERFORD

We start at one of the more popular spots in the Sound, an area that offers a variety of fish to area residents.

The reef lies just south of Waterford and is often visited by the Sunbeam Fleet that sails out of Capt. John's Sport Fishing Center just inside the Niantic River in Waterford. Four boats are available for all kinds of use. The queen of the fleet is the headboat "Sunbeam Express," a 149 passenger, 100-foot long beauty.

Captain John Wadsworth shared some of his knowledge about the reef as well as several other waters that his boats fish. If you find a lot of boats here you may have to drift for your fish, but John prefers to troll and his primary target is striped bass.

He likes to pull wire on his 42-foot fishing boat when he only has a small party on board. The boat can carry 15 but if a half-dozen or so patrons hired the boat, this is a good way to please them all.

Follow the tide, don't work across it, and work your lure. His favorite is the 1.4-ounce Shovel Nose or Smilin' Bill with a piece of pork rind added for more action. Carry a variety of pork rind colors and change them if you don't get enough action. Sometimes this is all you need.

Clearly, the main target is striped bass each spring, and then again in the fall, but since this is a "reef," an area that has a rocky bottom, you can expect to produce a nice catch of porgies and some blackfish when the water starts to warm up.

TIP: If you want a shot at the biggest 'tog around, get your boat set up over some rocks on a moving tide and fish the stern of the boat. Use two standard blackfish hooks, but only one bait. Pick a green crab with orange claws and break them off. Put each hook into and out separate vacated leg holes. You may only get a few bites each day, but they should be from big "slipperies." Just make sure to stick it to 'em good and reel fast!

Bonito and false albacore move onto Bartlett Reef each September and generally stay around for a month. You can catch them on bait but jigging will account for even more and some stripers will also be competing for the metal.

Over the rockiest chunks you can read on your machine, look for porgies here in late summer. A simple piece of clam is all you need, what folks call "Sea clams," or "Skimmer clams," preferably fresh ones. Stripers love them also so make sure to keep your drag a bit open. That expected half-pound scup might instead be a 10-pound lineside.

2 — CABLE & ANCHOR/BUOY 28C — Norwalk

Norwalk is the general vicinity, but truthfully, unless you have a good navigational chart and map, you won't find this site on virtually any standard map or Atlas. And because of that, I am truly indebted to Captain Sal Tardella of My Bonnie Charters for sharing his knowledge with me about one of his favorite spots.

"My Bonnie" sails out of South Norwalk off I95, and you can book a trip with him on his custom 25-foot boat by calling 1 203-866-6313.

Sailing out of a private marina on Village Creek, Norwalk, Sal fishes in April for schoolie stripers and he gets them in the warmer waters of the surrounding power plants. The Manresa plant in Norwalk is immediately adjacent to his marina, and the Northport "stacks" are directly across the Sound at a distance of 11.7 miles. Yet a third power plant is at nearby Bridgeport, about 13 miles to the northeast.

He catches bass in these areas by throwing a quarter-ounce white "Lima bean" bucktail jig with chartreuse Mr. Twister. Throw out as far as you can and bounce bottom slowly back to the boat, jigging all the way back. On anchor, an alternative method involves using a whole sandworm single hooked through its head on a 2/0 hook with only a little split shot to take the bait down. In modest tide, the worm will get to bottom and swim naturally.

But come mid-May on, it's off to 28C/Cable & Anchor, so to

Here's Capt. Sal Tardella with a 33 inch striper —
typical of what he catches at Cable & Anchor.

reach it, find Green's Ledge Light off Norwalk, and on a compass reading of 180 degrees, head three to four miles south to get there. Two spots that are nearby Cable & Anchor are:

1. Due south of the buoy until you are in 39-45 feet of water, and if that isn't productive, continue in the same direction until you are over 50-55 feet.

2. If this area is still slow, head northeast of the buoy to 40-45 feet of water and start fishing.

What's at and around Cable & Anchor in May? Striped bass, some of the bigger kind, as well as medium and large bluefish, that's what! He sets an anchor and gets a chum slick working quickly.

Capt. Sal mixes small bits of bunker with seawater and bottled bunker oil in a five-gallon bucket. A good long handled ladle is needed to mix and dispense the brew.

TIP: Well do I remember using a short ladle with too gooey chum years ago and I wound up hitting my friend in the face with the half that remained in the can on the back swing — he was not happy! Don't make it too thick — it sticks!

Chum heavily until the fish start to bite and then cut back to a modest sprinkle. Your best action should occur during the first two hours of a dropping tide.

Sal uses a 6/0 hook on 40 lb. test shock leader rather than on wire, with a three-ounce or heavier sinker bringing the bait down on a fish-finder rig.

3 — CAPTAINS ISLANDS — GREENWICH

Due south of Greenwich Harbor, is Captain Harbor and south of there by a bit are Captain's Islands. This is just a little to the east of the New York State Line in Portchester. Great Captain's Island is identified by name on many maps but you may have to look harder to find Little Captain's Islands nearby.

Not an island, but a real Captain, is Bryan Hocking of the charter craft Deborah Ann III out of Stamford. Bryan has had his license since 1980 but has been on the water for many years. He was helping operate the Admiral's Barge years ago in Florida when then Vice-President Hubert Humphrey was on board and the only sailfish that Admiral Brush ever got on the "barge" was reeled in by Humphrey, not by Brush!

The Deborah Ann can be reached at 1-203-792-2277 and is situated off exit 7, Atlantic Street on I95 at the Harbor Square Marina, 700 Canal Street, Stamford.

Bryan likes to fish the Islands for fluke mostly, but he also tries north of them off the racing buoys that are mid-sound.

His fluke fishing involves a single 2/0 hook with a 3-foot leader attached to a 3-way swivel. He uses anywhere from 2-6 ounces of lead depending on tide. The lighter the sinker he uses to drift with and still bounce along bottom, the better.

Hocking prefers a long squid strip with spearing added. I remember a conversation we had at the New Jersey Fisherman Magazine some years ago about which do you put on first, "white bait" or fish?

TIP: Since this is my book, do it my way! Put your strip bait on first and then the little fish. I really think that my production numbers are better this way than if I head-hooked the spearing first and then the squid.

Seriously, try a 5-6 inch length with it tapering down from a half-inch wide to a fine point at the end. Slit that end which provides an additional attraction when the bait is moving along the bottom.

And if you like bluefish, that area north of Captain's Islands we talked about before, off the racing buoys, is a super area. The Deborah Ann likes to drift with a double-hooked rig onto which Bryan adds, when available, a live bunker. They use wire leader with the hooks four inches apart, head hooking with the first hook and then sticking the trail hook just forward of the tail.

Blues for action and fluke for the frying pan, nice!

4 — CHARLES ISLAND/MILFORD POINT

The Governor mentioned weakfish in his foreword. This is one of the areas of the Sound where weakies have made a comeback. They are not the main goal here, but it is good to know that sea trout are back in the Sound again.

Milford Point is at the southern end of Milford Harbor, which is where the salt starts to enter the Housatonic River. If only for the sake of accuracy, let's say that Milford Point lies just within New Haven County. Up the coast of the sound from Milford Point in an easterly direction will be found Charles Island, straight out from Fort Trumball. Between the Point and the Island is where fine fishing is available.

The Island section of this stretch is better for stripers than blues as a rule, with more bluefish than bass at the Point, but we will talk about both since they are so close to each other. And to add to the confusion but to also give you more opportunity, remember that the mouth of the Housatonic is at Milford Harbor where many a good-sized striped bass can often be caught. Check out Milford Harbor later in this chapter for more details.

Striped bass will try to beat out the weakfish that you may be after if you are using a whole sandworm, but, hey, you catch what you gotta' catch, right?

TIP: Drift near the island early in the morning with a light rig and a long leader. Your sinker too should be on a long drop of say two feet below your three-way. The hook leader could be as long as five feet. First put on a strawberry colored plastic worm (six-inch) and then add a big, juicy sandworm onto your light shanked blue striper hook in size 2/0. Hope that a bluefish doesn't eat it and chop you off. Whether your catch is a striper or a sea trout, this style works very well.

Besides striped bass, bluefish, and the occasional weakie, a good number of fluke come into these grounds each summer too so if you want variety, try to drift with a strip of squid and a live killy ("mummie") for a flattie.

5 — DUCK ISLAND — Clinton — Westbrook

Duck Island is situated between Clinton and Westbrook, and is straight offshore of Grove Beach Point. If you have a seaworthy boat in the Patchogue River at Westbrook, just exit the river and head due south until you get there.

The main target is striped bass at the Island, with some bluefish mixed in. Stripers are caught in good number and size from mid-May through the end of September.

Generally speaking, you will catch many more stripers here than blues but bluefish from 2-10 pounds are not uncommon, especially in early July.

There are some tidal rips in and around the island so if you are alone in a small boat, make sure you know what you are doing here. If you get caught in a heavy rip you could flip with ease.

Take advantage of the rip though, if you are capable of doing so, by fishing its edge and letting the tide movement bring you into and out of the churning water.

You will see the rip with ease. Work the side of the island that has the tide taking you away. Come up pretty close, reading your depth record carefully, and let the current take you into deeper water.

While the standard rig for water that chugs like the Race, etc., is a drail with double-hooked herring, one of the main reasons for doing that is to hang bait without a long leader getting stuck into your neighbor's line two feet away on a head boat.

TIP: If you are in your own boat, or maybe a charter craft that you are sharing with one or two people, try a heavy enough sinker to take you to bottom with a three way swivel, off of which your three foot leader's hook has a double lip-hooked live eel on. This is great for bigger striped bass. If you get chopped off by a blue, that wasn't a good idea and you didn't hear about it here!

6 — FISHERS ISLAND SOUND —
Groton — Stonington

Offshore between Groton and Stonington, Fishers Island runs from west to east following those two towns, and is the largest area of saltwater we will talk about in this book. Clearly, it is more than a mouthful and deserves far more space than I will give it. To learn about this water far better, you may want to charter a boat.

Half of the Sound lies in New London County and the remainder is in Suffolk County, N. Y. It is at this line that several islands will appear. If you see three hunks of land near each other at the western side, you are in New York waters and you must know and obey any special regulations that exist there. Fluke are present in substantial number so, again, know the law!

TIP: Capt. Charlie Selby of Wildwood, N. J. once told me that he had his mate cut off and change each fluke hook daily, never using anything but a gold "English" style. He felt that a clean gold hook gave his customers the best chance at catching what they call "flounder" down there. My own preference is to use the same hook, a Mustad model #37162, but I use one much smaller than other folks use, a size #4. Always carrying a box of loose hooks. If an undersized fish swallows the hook, I cut it off and release it. The fish will live and I then just tie another hook on my leader. This small hook will present your bait far better to fluke, in the rivers or sound.

Fishers Island Sound marks the exitway from Connecticut to Rhode Islands waters from which you can reach Block Island and then the further off and fish-rich waters of Montauk. Lots of boats will take this ride for cod, tuna, etc. Most of the bigger head and charter boats from the Niantic, Thames and Mystic Rivers have easy access to such grounds.

The south side of the island, in New York water, is a particularly hot area for fluke. Wilderness Point, near its western end, is one of the best flattie spots of all. Technically, you are now in Block Island Sound. Bluefish are swimming right along where these fluke are, though, so if you get chopped off you may want to switch over.

Isabella Beach in Block Island Sound also has good fluke fishing in mid-summer.

It is not uncommon to catch a harbor bluefish on a non-weighted bucktail tied above the sinker and a good-sized fluke on the bottom hook, two at a time here.

The northern side of the island, most of which is in Connecticut water, holds quite a few rocky reef sections that are super spots for porgies and blackfish, with good numbers of sea bass common too. One such spot is the Latimer Reef. Latimer is marked by a bell buoy southeast of Stonington. Another hunk of hard bottom is called the Seaflower Reef.

Most anglers use squid strips on a two hook rig but I prefer to

*Bonnie Tardella nailed this 4.56 pound fluke in 9/99
on the Long Island side of L.I.S.*

use skimmer clam (not the stringy stuff that wraps around the side of both shells). That makes good decoration. Instead go with the large "center cut" of clam meat, commonly called the tongue. If the fish are small, cut this into two halves and cut your baits from each part. The bigger clams have a tongue that is often too thick to cut your baits out of for hand-sized scup.

Instead of tying both hooks off to fall below the sinker, rig one that drops to three or four inches above the lead and a single hook below. Use a small strip of filleted mackerel on the top hook and clam below. The strip often will account for some of your bigger sea bass.

7 — HARKNESS PARK & REEF — New London

Flatfish own this area. And if it is important for you to know the difference between a fluke and a flounder, forget that business about eyes on which side. Just stick your finger in their mouth. If you bleed, it's a fluke.

Whether your goal is one or the other, the Sunbeam Fleet from Waterford can bring you to them, and Captain John Wadsworth shared some knowledge about one of his favorite areas for both fish, from shore or boat.

He told me that shore anglers can find plenty of action in Harkness Memorial State Park and while winter flounder are not found in great numbers in the state, it is a fine way to get out into the fresh air on an early spring morning. They start to bite inshore first and then those that are in the Sound feed later, and are joined by flatties that begin to move offshore too.

Capt. John (his boat's run out of "Captain John's Sport Fishing Center," by the way) suggests using sandworms or fresh clams, but a good alternate is mussel. He recommends a light spinning rod and reel combination with just enough lead to hold bottom. At times he feels that a spreader will assist, with two small flounder hooks tied on.

TIP: My personal favorite is a #10 Mustad model #79580. It's small and skinny and easy to swallow. If the flounder is undersized, simply cut your line and throw it back. The hook will rust out quickly.

If a channel is near, try to fish its edge. Let the bait lay on bottom but keep a tight line. When you feel or see a bite, lift up slowly to set the hook. A quick jerk may take the bait away from the fish before it has the hook in its mouth. The slow lift should get it to clamp down.

As the flounder start to feed in the Sound later in the spring, you can find them on a reef just offshore of Harkness and west of that reef but north of a Green Can is another good spot. You have a shot at more active fish now. Those that feed earliest really prefer the softest of baits but later on, they are not so finicky.

Once the water warms up, it's time to fish for fluke. Try just off the park or at the other flounder spots we just went into.

John suggests using a three-way swivel with light weight. He favors a three-foot leader with spinner and 5/0 hook. He likes the hook to have nylon or bucktail to add to the attraction already created by the spinner. Put a strip of squid on the hook and then a "mummie" (killy). If the drift is slow, lift from time to time to remove grass and add still more life to the bait. Hop on board one of John's boats for a half-day of drifting for them!

8 — HATCHETT REEF — Old Lyme

About halfway between the Connecticut and Niantic Rivers are Sound View Beach and Hatchett Point. Straight out from this land is one of the best offshore waters of the Sound, called Hatchett Reef. Weekly reports from the State are filled with tales of fine action out here.

There are some humps that rise up a little south of the Reef which hold striped bass. They like this area and are found in sizable number here.

In addition to striped bass, the reef contains sufficient rock to attract porgies in the summer and fall, with some blackfish thrown in too.

TIP: Remember those sea clams we talked about? If you are on the Reef and the tide is slack, have a supply of clam bellies in your bait container. Have some very light gauze material with you and a good pair of scissors. For porgies, use small hooks and a hunk of belly. Striper lovers should go with two clam bellies on a bigger hook. If you want to keep the bait on longer, just wrap a little section of the gauze around the bait and tie it together.

It's work, yes, but it works!

Come fall, the scup, porgies and stripers have company. False albacore are on the reef too with bonito.

9 — LONG SAND SHOAL —
Old Saybrook — Lyme

Among the many dedicated employees of the Division is Ernie Beckwith who is in charge of their Marine Fisheries Division. Ernie shared some of the knowledge he has gleaned over the years with me about this super site.

The Connecticut River leaves it shoreline at Old Saybrook/Old Lyme, and heads out into the Sound. As the current brings water out, with it comes sediment which, over the years, created Long Sand Shoal. The more movement, the greater the change and shift of the shoal but by and large, here is where it is:

The shoal runs east and west, starting a little to the east of the river's Old Lyme side, and ranges as far to the west off Old Saybrook as four or five miles.

The shoal itself is 1½ to 2 miles due south of the inlet, and has a variety of depths, depending on buildup. You can find 12-18 feet of water but 20-28 foot depths are generally better places to find action. Ernie told me that offshore of the shoal you can find anywhere from 50-110 feet of water and when the tide is cranking, lots of fish are in the rip created by the movement.

Stripers are common, and although most of them are not real "cows," a 10-20-pounder is not uncommon. The two other species that are very common are bluefish and fluke.

TIP: If in your own boat, instead of bait for stripers or blues, try an Ava style jig. While many of these jigs are dressed already with hard plastic tubes, I prefer to have a package of black grape jelly worms with me instead. My jig of choice has a clean undressed hook and I slide the head of the plastic worm up the shank to the eye of my hook, leaving ¾ of it dangling. Cast out as far as you can. When it hits bottom, reel as fast as possible with a quick-retrieve reel. You cannot get the lure away fast enough from a blue or striper — it will beat you & hook up!

The east end of the shoal offers some of the better fluke catches in more shallow water early, but as the summer progresses, head towards the western side and off into deeper water. This is a traditional pattern with fluke. They are generally in shallower

*Here's famous writer Tom Boyd
with a beautiful striped bass he beat on a fly.*

water early and deeper late. However, if you are in shallow water
and feel your sinker and it is cold, get deeper to warmth.

You can tell when the water is not warm enough for your fluke,
even if they are feeding. Their bite will be not much more than a
hold. Drifting along, if you feel a little dead weight, that might be a
chilly fluke hanging on instead of seaweed.

10 — MILFORD HARBOR

Unless a stiff south wind is blowing, Milford Harbor is a pretty good place for you to fish at from your small boat. Up above, we discussed Charles Island/Milford Point, which is an area far larger than the Harbor. Milford Harbor involves a public fishing area on its west side at Silver Sands State Park, which is a little south of Fort Trumball. The shoreline squeezes in from west and east in the Harbor from Silver Sands to Welches Point.

Since Milford Point is southwest of the Harbor at the mouth of the Housatonic, and is due north of Charles Island, add this to your go to list if you fish those sections as well. Once again, it is quite well sheltered from all but the worst of winds, and offers very good striped bass action.

Since stripers are the primary target in the Harbor, let's get a bit more specific. First, the north end, closest to land, is usually best. And nighttime is the right time many times.

TIP: If you have a well lit boat and can anchor out safely at night, try this style — Buy a dozen sandworms and put a hi-low rig together. A dropper loop with a six-inch leader gets one sandworm on the hook. It should take you down to three feet above the sinker. Now on your second hook, one with a two-foot leader, add worm #2.

Drop down to bottom and wait 'em out. If you have access to grass shrimp, feed some out overboard every ten to fifteen minutes. Dead ones are okay but those that float won't work, because they need to sink to near where your worms are.

Hickory Shad are the other fish that are found in Milford Harbor in good numbers. Catch some and chunk them in the summer as your second bait of choice for bass.

11 — NEW HAVEN HARBOR

Along the entire shoreline of the state, far and away the widest harbor of all is New Haven Harbor. While it may not have been thought of as a super place to fish in when a Naval Reserve Training Ship, the U. S. S. Coates was stationed there back in the 50's, it is now!

There are quite a few places in the river that you can either stand at and fish from shore or launch your boat. Standing room can be found on the East Haven side at East Shore Park on Woodward Avenue; Fort Hale Park, also along Woodward Avenue; the end of Cove Place (where a car-topper can be put in as well); and out near the Sound, at Lighthouse Point Park which has a ramp and standing room.

Over on the west side of the river is a whole string of sites (the boat ramp off April Street in West Haven is a fine launch site). Nearby, a stand and fish spot is at Sandy Point off of Beach Street. There are at least six access piers or docks ranging out to the Sound from there.

As with several of the other harbors, New Haven is visited by some very large ships so don't anchor out and fall asleep at night. In fact, if you are going to sit on the hook during the daytime, make sure your engine starts the first time you turn the key. Have someone else to pull the anchor, just in case you need to move quickly!

All four of the targeted fish appear simultaneously in early June, so get your boat ready to fish by mid-May!

Besides stripers and blues, and your good old standby fluke, weakies have appeared in New Haven Sound for the past few years and chances are they may be here to stay.

TIP: The cleanest and most simple rig imaginable is what you want for weakfish. Two leaders, two feet long, are tied into your line off of dropper loops. Place one 3-4 feet above the sinker and number two goes in right at the sinker knot. Use a claw/beak style hook in size 1/0. (Smaller if the sea trout are smallish). Cut clean strips of squid in three inch lengths, only a half-inch wide where you single hook it, and tapered down to a point. These strips will flutter in the tide and a double-header is not beyond expectation. Of course a blue might take the top one and a fluke the bottom but, do what you gotta'do.

Drifting the Harbor is generally best, because there is so much water to cover. But if you catch a few fish and can identify your "hole," punch in the numbers quickly if you have Loran. Chances are good that this spot might produce day after day on a similar

Our own Troy Klauder holding the 36 inch striper he caught at Lighthouse Beach on a giant sandworm. Look up our friend Troy at his website: www.redmoonguides.com for some good stuff.

tide. (Just add ¾ to one hour later for each following day).

Perhaps the hottest of hot chunks of the harbor is found at Sandy Point, one of the areas we talked about on the west side earlier. This is a natural holding area for passing blues and stripers because it protrudes out nearly halfway into the Harbor. So if you want the best of the best, for all the fish around, try at or off Sandy Point!

12 — NIANTIC BAY/BLACK POINT

The Bay has as its borders East Lyme and Waterford, the same as Niantic River does which we get into later. More commonly called Black Point at times, for now we will use Niantic Bay as the name of this area, but I will also cross-reference it under Black Point too.

Black Point is that tip of land at the southwestern edge of the Bay, and fishing in and around this protrusion is often very successful, with fluke as the target more than anything else is. Captain John Wadsworth of the Sunbeam Fleet likes to work the mouth of the bay itself for fluke.

If you head across the bay in a northeasterly direction, you will get to the Millstone Power Plant, another fine spot to try.

Between the Point and the Plant is the Bay, and this water may be the best place in the state to go after weakfish. Some sea trout from 20 to 30 inches are caught along with fluke on the same drift.

TIP: They are not called "weak" fish for nothing. In case you have never tried to simply lift one into your boat, don't start doing it now. Have a large net on board and slip it into the water and let the fish slide headfirst into the opening. Weakfish have lips that often open little holes out of which your hook could easily fall on a lift. Therefore, net them all, please.

Lots of bluefish come into the bay itself and over towards the west side at Black Point, the best of the striped bass action can often by found. Fluke are out in the open water of the bay and as it starts getting colder in early September, they move out towards the Sound further into deeper water.

As you will read in the Fresh/Brackish Waters chapter, the Niantic River attracts schools of Hickory shad. It would be a good idea to have some fresh ones on hand for bay fishing. Since they are a natural bait, a boneless chunk may be just what the doctor ordered for blues and bass. In fact, while fluke and weakfish prefer tapered bait, a shad hunk would also be gobbled by both of them as well. You may be able to catch some shad in the bay in the fall.

Come mid to late October, the warm water of the Millstone Power Plant area attracts false albacore and bonito. By the way, if you are from Florida, here's a lesson for you. What you guys call "Bonito" are what we call "Albacore." Down south, bonito are considered trash fish because their purple meat is awful on the table, but that is NOT a bonito. It is instead the false albacore that we like to catch up here but usually release alive.

*Molly Northrop caught this little striper off Norwalk Islands
in 1997. Her proud pop Jeff told me she catches bigger ones now
and wins sailboat events too.*

13 — NORWALK ISLANDS

Back into Norwalk Harbor are at least two boat launch sites.
They are off Seaview Avenue. One is called Transient Boat Docks
and the other is named Veterans Memorial Park. But if you would
like to get closer to the outlet of the Harbor, and nearer yet to the
Norwalk Islands, put in at Calf Pasture Beach Road. Non-residents
must pay a parking fee here.

*Capt. Jeff Northrop of Westport Outfitters said that Reed Whittle
(holding fish) released this 16½ pound false albacore
that he caught on a Clouser minnow —
at the time, it would have been a 20 pound class world record!*

From the east at the Saugatuck River back westerly towards the Norwalk Islands is where you want to make your fluke drifts in the summer, but in May, you might catch some winter flounder while on anchor inshore of the islands.

TIP: A whole string of islands are found offshore of Norwalk. Fog builds up here quickly and if you don't have radar to see the islands, at least know your tides and try to stay in the navigation channels.

My map shows six islands with specific names and several others that are simply there, with no names at all. What you need to know is that these are natural feeding grounds for a wide variety of game fish and we will shortly turn to one of the top area experts for his expertise here, in particular, his skill with the light wand!

Species caught in and around the Islands include bass and blues in the summer, with weakies as well, and more fluke than anything at times. Sometimes the better bluefish bite comes closer to the Harbor with more bass around the islands. Come fall, bonito and false albacore show up and break many an unsuspecting angler's line.

My favorite fish is a hybrid striped bass/white bass, and I hope that they get some soon in Connecticut's lakes. Until then, picture the wonderful fight of a bonito and you've got the saltwater equivalent. They hardly ever jump, but change direction on a dime, and dig deep for all their worth. They are wonderful fighting fish! Line shy, they prefer a small hook and bait, and make excellent table fare as well, with good tasting white meat.

Captain Jeff Northrop may be the best known saltwater flyfisherman in New England and has several boats available for hire. He sails out of the Saugatuck River and is only minutes away from the islands. His brochure says that there are actually 18 islands in all. Call him at 1-203-226-1915 to arrange for a charter.

And now let Jeff do the talking: "Starting in the early spring you can expect to stalk migrating bass in and around the mouths of the seven rivers that flow into the island chain. As warmer weather arrives, so do the schools of larger bass. These fish, after making their long run from the Hudson, are looking to gorge on the abundant sand eel hatch that takes place on our shallow water sand flats. When June arrives, the bass are joined on the flats by huge daisy chaining bluefish. These spawning females, ranging between 15 and 20 pounds, will aggressively take large deceivers, producing tarpon-like jumps and excitement. In the fall the striped bass and bluefish, along with bonito and false albacore, feed non-stop in anticipation of the migration south. With wheeling birds above and pods of bait below, the stage is set for some of the most intense action available, the Fall Blitz" — wow!

14 — OBSTRUCTION BUOY — Norwalk

No fool he, I found Captain Sal Tardella of "My Bonnie Charters" in Sebastian, Florida when I spoke to him in the winter that I put the book together.

"My Bonnie" sails out of Norwalk to spots on both sides of the Sound. Sal has fished the Sound for 30 years, at first from Rye, N. Y. and now out of Norwalk. He fishes the Norwalk Islands that we talked at length about already. In addition, he visits all the close-in spots along his coast, as well as running across to the Long Island side to Cold Spring, Sunken Meadow, etc.

Among his favorite areas in between the two coasts are Cable & Anchor/Buoy 28C, which we went into earlier, and The Obstruction Buoy. About that hot spot called "O.B."

We took you directly to the Cable & Anchor above. From that buoy, head SW 190-200 degrees for about one mile. OB is a can-type structure. When you're at this point, you will see the Coast Guard Station on a hill due south at Eaton's Neck on Long Island.

Now head NW for about 100 feet. Your recorder will show 20-35 feet. Head west slowly, and your bottom will crash down from 30 to 90 feet. Your machine will show the slope. Most fish stay from the top 30 feet of water to halfway down the slope at 60 feet, hanging around for a meal. Sal said that you should see other boats around the OB but if not, I hope that you can find it with his fine directions.

His 250 HP Yamaha Outboard brings him out to the Obstruction Buoy quickly and his style of fishing involves bait, bait, and more bait. While others will fish jigs, My Bonnie targets striped bass and bluefish with bunker chunks and catches plenty of each that way.

If you have access to fresh mossbunker (menhaden), they make the best bait of all. Even if it is frozen bait, the chunk you use gives off an enticing odor to nearby fish. They will get near to your boat if you start to throw chum overboard in sizable portions as soon as your boat starts to settle down on the anchor.

If you have set up well on the edge of the slope, you may find that your first drop down will get whacked even before you reach bottom. It is late Spring, so if you intend to keep some fish for a meal, make sure you have a big cooler with plenty of ice. It is easy for the flesh of a blue or bass to soften and get ruined if not put on ice immediately after hitting the deck.

TIP: In our freshwater section we discuss a few lakes that contain smelt. They generally bite early in the year, before Capt. Tardella is out at the OB, but if you do fish any of these lakes and catch some smelt, save some for bait! Freeze them six to a baggie, and take a bag or two out to sea with you. While they don't offer the odor of a bunker chunk, their flash and shape may be your best bait!

15 — OCEAN BEACH STATE PARK —
New London

The Sunbeam Fleet of boats out of Waterford often makes the short trip east to Ocean Beach State Park for fluke, and Captain John Wadsworth told me that this is a fine place to catch them. Of course his boats also do well in the summer close by around the Two Tree Channel between Two Tree Island and Waterford, and other nearby spots.

Ocean Beach is out towards the southwestern end of New London Harbor, just before Harkness Memorial State Park. It is a popular area for bathers, but let's try drifting offshore for summer flounder instead of swimming today.

Headboat fishing often involves luck. I hate to tell you how many times the biggest fluke on the boat is caught by someone who has never fished a party boat in their lives. While they may be good in freshwater, chances are at least equal that they never fished anywhere!

You see, one of the secrets to catching fluke, some of the biggest around, is to NOT respond right away. Experienced anglers set way too often on fluke, and miss many of them. The bait is long and the boat is moving. This doesn't give the fish enough time to swallow the hook and when many anglers feel their first good tug, they set, and come up blank.

Beginners may respond, but they may also have slack line and not know the difference so by the time they realize that something is at the other end, they get the fish!

Captain Wadsworth pointed out that the fish are found on sandy bottom. At times, ribs in the sand make you feel that you are bouncing over a washboard, but a bite is a bite, and there is a difference.

TIP: Feel your sinker carefully the first time you reel up to check your bait. If it is cold, follow this concept carefully to catch fluke. In cold water, they will mouth a bait that is close by. With a delicate touch, you can feel the difference barely between sinker alone and sinker with something hanging on. Now open your reel and let five feet out, quickly! Lift the rod an inch or two when the line tightens. If you still feel more weight than normal, let out another five feet and do it again. By this time, the fish probably got the whole bait down and it's time to slam! Reel fast and steady. If you have light tackle, don't tighten down completely on the drag because bigger fluke will try to take a dive for the bottom when they see the boat. Wait for the mate to net the fish. Don't take its head out of the water. Just slide it in headfirst!

16 — THE RACE — Eastern Sound

Not in Connecticut waters at all, The Race is actually a bit to the Long Island side of the Sound, but you will probably see more Connecticut boats fishing it than New Yorkers! For example, even though I lived in New York for many years, I never fished the very popular spot then. And just about every time I visit with my family in Gales Ferry, we make a trip to The Race for blues and stripers. And without fail, every single time that I have been there, we have all caught fish!

So for your best chance at action on a big boat, hop on board any of the craft that sail out of The Niantic, Thames, or Mystic Rivers. It's less than an hour away.

This is, by far, the best place in the entire Sound to catch striped bass and bluefish, but it also a very dangerous area if you are not capable of handling some of the wildest water around.

The Race is not a place for a small boat. It is, on the other hand, a spot that experienced and licensed skippers know like the back of their hand. You see, the water crashes around this way and that, and it is difficult to maneuver through with a small boat. You yourself will feel the motion, which is why so many fish are here. When the tides are banging against each other, smaller fish get disoriented and that is when the big guys eat!

*My grandson Joe Morea with his first "No Help" blue,
caught at the Race on the Mi-Joy.*

I've seen the Hel-Cat, Sunbeam Express, and the Mi-Joy 747
out here, among others. For now, let's hear from Captain Joe
Devine of the Mi-Joy in his own words, and if they don't get your
juices going, take up golf.

"It's 6:00 in the morning and the big diesel engines of the
Mi-Joy 747, skippered by Captain Paul Brockett, are pulling away
from their berth on the Waterford side of the Niantic River. They're
heading south. Heading for The Race. The Race is the opening on
the eastern end of the Sound where billions of gallons of water

*Joe Devine of the Mi-Joy sent this photo in
of a beautiful striper taken on his boat at the Race.*

rush through on each tide. Not only does the change of water carry in a fresh supply of oxygen-rich water, but also new supplies of bait and fish.

On deck, the crew is preparing bait, handing out rods, and giving classes in Bluefish 101. After a short time, we arrive at the Race. Capt. Paul is looking around for a shoal of fish. On any given day, the fish can be in water as shallow as 40 feet or on the bottom in nearly 300 feet. What makes The Race so special is that it has very hard bottom with rocky peaks, boulders, and very steep banks — the perfect place for blues and bass to ambush baitfish.

Tackle for The Race should include heavy boat rods and reels capable of holding 300 yards of 50-pound test monofilament. The primary way to catch fish in The Race is a drail rig: a sinker with an eye on each end with a length of chain, a 9/0 hook, and a duolock snap. This rig, fished with the boat supplied bait, works great, because with all the lines in the water, the Mi-Joy 747 is its own school of bait." Capt. Joe also jigs but let's stay with bait:

"The captain blows the horn and bait drops to the bottom. The trick to The Race, however, is finding it and getting out of its way. Once you hit bottom, you need to engage the reel and keep your bait a few turns off the rocks so you don't get snagged as the boat drifts towards the fish. The Race is quick water and the fish are always on the go, so anchoring is no option. The trip revolves around a series of drifts, and as the boat passes through the fish, rods are quickly bent from the power of fighting bass and blues. Now anglers young and old struggle to convince their opponents that swimming to the surface is the way to go."

"Soon fish circle at the surface and the mates hear cries for the gaff. The mates use their long, hooked poles to bring in the blues and (as required by law), sturdy nets to bring in the striped bass. The horn blows again and everyone pulls in their lines. It's time to set for another drift. With the help of a Loran and a GPS, the captain runs back up to the same spot and sets the drift again. If the trend continues, a trip can produce many bass and blues."

Joe continued, but I had to stop copying his words because they brought back too many exciting memories and I wanted to head to Casa Morea/Luftglass and grab my family and get out to The Race IMMEDIATELY, but I had to finish the book!

TIP: You can certainly bring your own rod and reel, but leave the skinny pole at home. Forget the light rod. You must have a sturdy stick or else the ten guys you tangle with may want to chuck you overboard!

17 — WEST BREAKWALL — STONINGTON

It's after 5 p.m. and nearly everyone has headed back to the barn. That is when Captain David Orlowski runs one of his two charter boats out of Noank for a shot at a combination of quiet with excitement mixed in.

The quiet is found in the early evening when the wind eases up and boat waves are gone. The excitement? Well, how about catching stripers and blues that are clearly visible on the top, smashing into helpless baitfish?

Dave fishes an area between White Rock to the east of him, and

Capt. David Orlowski ran his smaller boat
to produce this quality striped bass.

over further to the east at Stonington Harbor, off the West
Breakwall of the Harbor, thus the name of this spot. There is a
fishing pier in Stonington Harbor where you can catch fish from at
times too, but if they don't come right by you, it can be like a kid
looking at a cake in a locked bakery. On the other hand, Dave sees,
moves towards, and catches fish most of the time. (The pier is in
Stonington, on Pearl Street at the "Town Dock").

But back to sea on "The Last Resort," one of Orlowski's craft.
This water is pretty shallow, and since you won't be on a crowded
boat, go light if you want, but your rod tip needs to be slow action

to cast a heavy lure. Dave looks for birds to help locate the fish but if the water is as calm as it often gets, you will see the fish rising. Watch for a moment if you can stand not casting right away, and move slowly towards the area you think the fish are swimming to. These will be two feet long on up, and there will be plenty of them to catch. Rig a medium spinning rod with 15-pound mono and have a heavy lure on to cast out to where the fish are rising. Bomber lures or bucktail jigs are two of his favorites.

TIP: If you can work in close without making much noise, you can even hit them on a fly rod bucktail.

18 — BUOY 32A STAMFORD HARBOR

The last of our "Best" salty waters can be found about four miles out from Stamford Harbor, and Captain Bryan Hocking of the Deborah Ann III told me about it.

Bryan works just east of 32A for bluefish. 32A is mid-sound, between Stamford and Bayville Beach on the Long Island side.

Hocking trolls when the opportunity presents itself, and also does well jigging, but his favorite style is fishing with bait, and 32A is the spot he prefer over all.

When the Deborah Ann leaves her dock and heads out, he always looks for schools of bunker, either on top, or with his fish finder. Bryan will have several outfits rigged with weighted treble hooks to snag a supply of bait with.

TIP: Some people snag with two or three plain trebles above a sinker. Bryan's style is better. The weighted treble is all you need and it gets right into the bait instead of having to make an arc as is needed with a swinging sinker.

If menhaden aren't available Bryan always has frozen bait on hand. In addition to bunker, he sometimes carries mackerel and butterfish.

Bryan anchors up and has several customers drop their lines to the bottom, but has a few let out line with no sinker at all into the tide, being careful to not have them tangle up. He makes his own rigs with an 8-10 inch 80 lb. test wire leader, and an 8/0 hook, with a barrel swivel to tie the line onto. Again, tied straight to your line

*Skipper Bryan Hocking of the Deborah Ann III
sent in this fine example of what he produces at "32A."*

or adding a fish finder and 3-6 ounce sinker, depending on whether he wants the line up or down.

If he has live bunker, the style involves a double hook rig like we talked about back at Captain's Island.

HONORABLE MENTION

The Connecticut part of the Sound holds many other good waters too. To name just a few, we have:

- **Ran Island Reefs/Mystic — Stonington —** striped bass.
- **The Six-Mile Reef off of Clinton** for blues, bass, some fluke, and later — bonito and false albacore.
- **Sound View/White Sands Beach — Old Lyme,** for fluke.
- **Stratford Shoal/Middle Grounds —** blues, porgies, etc.

My grandson Joseph Morea is holding the 12 lb. bluefish
that his dad Greg caught on the Mi-Joy at the Race in 1993
as his sister Rebecca is standing by.

CHAPTER 2

Fresh / Brackish / Salt Rivers

19 — CONNECTICUT RIVER

We start with the biggest of all the rivers in the state, one that actually begins way up near the Canadian border in New Hampshire, from where it travels south where it enters the Long Island Sound, a distance of 410 miles.

Some say that the river got its name from members of the Algonquin federation. They called it Quinatucquet or Quinnetukut, both of which meaning "long tidal river." This is because the river runs tidal back as far north from the Long Island Sound as the Enfield Rapids.

Chosen as one of 14 "American Heritage Rivers," the Connecticut was the first major river in the country to be improved for transportation. (And I bet you thought it was the Mississippi, right?)

In order to assist both shad and salmon in migrating north to spawn, fish ladders have been erected at several points along the route north. They can be found in Vermont and Massachusetts.

The Connecticut River is one of the only bodies of water in the whole state that has a population of channel catfish, the biggest member of the catfish family by far in the state. Considered by many to be a "Game Fish," a 10-20 pounder is not uncommon at all.

*Craig Mergens at Riverfront Recaptue Inc., sent this photo to me
of an 8 year old with a beautiful smallmouth bass, caught 6/2/98
during a "Get Hooked On Fishing Not On Drugs" event
at Riverside Park on the Connecticut River.*

I was sent a copy of a booklet put out by the Connecticut Light
and Power Company from which I received lots of help. I suggest
you pick up a copy yourself. One day, when I get to know the river
better, I might just sit down and start to write a separate book,
which I will call "Gone Fishin'in the Connecticut River." If it hasn't
been written yet, such a book should be written, and I hope to be
able to write it for you. Look for it soon!

So until that day, let me try to take you down river from where it starts as freshwater in the state, until it gets brackish, and then finally out into the Sound. Along the way, you will have access to an incredible variety of fish. By the way, I am not about to lecture you on the safety of eating fish from the river. That is up to you, and you should check health advisories before doing so.

Some special rules apply to the river and let's go over a few before anything else.

Even though the river itself is not trout stocked, since so many trout streams eventually drop into it, please understand that, while there is no "Closed Season," you can only keep two trout per day and each must be at least 15 inches long. As for bass, large and smallmouth, the standard six fish, 12-inch limit applies.

American Shad fishing is open south of the Putnam Bridge to the Sound, from 6 a.m. on 4/1 to 6/30. Watch out for the 1,000-foot long nets that stretch across sections that are set for shad. Small floating lights are at each end.

You can get a serious headache trying to understand the herring rules but you need to know them — check 'em out!

Speed limits apply in varying degree so here I suggest you check the local regulation section of the Boater's Guide.

As you head down the river from where it leaves Massachusetts and comes into the north central tip of the state, let's find a few public fishing areas as well as public boat ramps. Clearly, I will not find all of each for you, but at least you will get a few to use.

Starting at the state line, first comes a public fishing area on its west side near Suffield. Next is the very popular ramp at Enfield, a mile northwest of the junction of US5 and I91. Take a left on Bridge Lane to Parson Road, where the ramp is on the right side. 20 can park here. It gets crowded during shad season.

As you get into brackish water, the next ramp is at the Route 291 Bridge south of Windsor at Wilson. It's at the Bissell Bridge that can be found east off Route 159, onto E. Barber Street.

A short distance further south are several in and around Hartford. One is at Jennings Road, Riverside Park and charges a fee. Another is the Charter Oak Landing off Reserve Rd.

Well south at Haddam Meadows State Park is a ramp on the west side and a public fishing area on the east. Just a little below that, at the mouth of the Salmon River off Route 149, 1½ miles north of the junction with Route 82 above E. Haddam, is a fee ramp that can accommodate 60 cars.

At the Route I95 Baldwin Bridge is a pay ramp on the western shore. It has handicap access and a 400-foot long fishing pier!! A boat launch is present and as many as 100 vehicles with trailers can park close by. It gets crowded!

TIP: Again, when I write the book I will give you a batch of them, but perhaps the most important one here is to tell you that state regulations demand that if you fish at or below the I95 Bridge, you must have a Freshwater License if you otherwise are required to have one in Connecticut.

Still more shore fishing can be done from the west side above Old Saybrook and on the eastern edge, at the Great Island Wildlife Area.

If you want a much more complete list of the access sites and ramps available in the brackish/salt waters of the river, write to the state for a copy of their Coastal Access Guide. It pinpoints sites for this river, as well as for nearly all of the other fresh to salt rivers I will be telling you about in the book!

We've gone over a lot of rules and regulations, and discussed history and where to launch, etc., now let's talk about the fishing itself, okay?

Reading from the data I got from the state, here's some things to whet your appetite — The river offers great variety. Bouncing around from one area to another and from one season to another — Largemouth bass are south of Hartford, with smallies north of Windsor. Calico bass are in the coves. White perch and carp are throughout.

Crappie are found in sizable numbers in White Oak and Wethersfield Coves each October. Try a tube jig for them. If you like channel catfish, work the upstream end of deep holding areas from April to June. Nothing beats a chunk of fresh herring or shad at that time.

Schoolie stripers are available the year-round with the largest fish coming in the spring and fall. Shad and herring are here, but watch those herring regulations, okay? In Windsor-Hartford, stripers and shad are found in the spring. The shad are both Hickory and American. A State Saltwater Record Hickory (2 pounds) was caught in 2000 by Carl Ponzillo and by the time you read this book, it may have already been smashed. The record freshwater American shad also came from the Connecticut. Back in 1981 Edward Cypus nailed a 9.4 pounder at Windsor.

Upstream of the E. Haddam Bridge is where you can get good catches of both white perch and eels. In the fall, you can find stripers, hickory shad, and even some bluefish and flounder are found this far up.

If you fish downstream of the Old Lyme Amtrak RR bridge at Old Saybrook, the coves and channel edge drop-offs hold northern pike. And the mouth of the river itself holds a wide variety of opportunities. Besides stripers and bluefish, how about trying to drift for fluke from the RR bridge to South Cove in season, or if the tide is very slow, doing the same thing in late autumn for winter flatties?

Besides both members of the shad family that are river record fish, the Connecticut also boasts other records. Can you just imagine the surprise felt by Bruce Kelly in 1995 when he found out that his 118.7 pound sandbar shark put him in the books? And in brackish water, the heaviest state white catfish, 12.12 pounds, was taken by John L. Shatas in 1999 at Middletown. Of course the 38½ pound carp caught by Stephen J. Woronecki at Hartford in 1995 got the record then, but lots of heavier carp are in a variety of Connecticut's waters. Fellow-members of the Carp Anglers Club have sworn me to secrecy about exact locations, but if you can find a warm water discharge you can even catch monster carp in the wintertime.

Some more stuff gleaned from the weekly fishing reports I got from the state showed that if you want channel catfish, try the waters of Portland and E. Haddam where James Thomas caught a 7.4 pound Mr. Whiskers in June of 2000. 3-6 pounders are commonplace around downed trees and in the deep pools from Middletown to Hartford.

Spring sees the winter flounder start and one day, they may be back in good numbers. You might hook up with a flounder with wings instead because a lot of skates are on hand also. Get a good, sharp cookie cutter and make your own "scallops" that way. Just don't try to sell them.

The Hamburg Cove offers fine white perch action late in April as a rule, and then the herring and striper runs begins. Use the biggest kind of swimming plug you can find for the stripers, one that matches the color of a herring. The little down river bass prefer bait.

As for shad, in addition to where we told you about, try the I91 Bridge up to the Enfield Dam in May. The water in and around Griswold Point is an area to work in the late spring. Stripers are featured and some flounder can be had too as the water warms up further and starts to chase them out. And then the fluke start up and take over. Try to fish a flood tide for fluke.

Bluefish join in and the crab trap brigade starts to do well from docks and piers, especially on slack water.

With warm water comes better smallmouth activity around Haddam and Enfield, and the largemouth lovers catch them well at Glastonbury/Wethersfield, plus Hartford. And although pike are taken in cold water too, they start attacking big white spinner baits near Haddam better than live bait as their metabolism warms.

Once the fluke season takes hold in July, count on some fine catches from the Dock and Dine Restaurant to the breakwaters. Again, flood is best. Our "scallop"/skates return in the early fall and are joined by other trash fish like sea robins. However, if you can avoid the spikes and have a sharp knife and the boat isn't rocking, fillet out a few strips off your sea robins for some of the best kind of doormat bait you can find. Make sure you have a double-hook rig and taper your bait. Cut some of the extra meat away so that your fillet can flutter well.

Bluefish are in and out on the tides, at the river mouth from Old Lyme Shores to the Westbrook beaches.

During the majority of the year you can catch smallies, large-mouth, crappie, pike, white perch, channel catfish, carp, etc., in much of the brackish waters. A good run of hickory shad returns in the fall around the DEP Marine Headquarters fishing pier and bulkhead, and the fall run of flounder starts up. Stripers are here too. Try a live eel for the bigger bass.

We talked above about a few big fish caught in the river. Here's a few more, and they were just some 2000 fish:

Joseph Sanservino caught a 4½ pound smallie that May. One weighing exactly the same was taken in June by Joseph Netolicky. Lynne Villano-Knecht caught a slab crappie — it weighed 2.4 pounds. A 41-inch, 21 pound northern pike came to the net that July. Add in large blues and stripers, with record carp lurking in hiding, and who knows what else, and the answer is clear-fish the Connecticut!

If you are looking for a guide to help you locate fish around the Enfield Dam, you might want to give a call to Jimmy McGillivray at J & J Outfitters (1-860-623-7335). The 7335 stands for "reel," and he reels in plenty of fish. Jimmy has taken lots of stripers in the 40's with largemouth and smallmouth bass plus northern pike the other fish that he concentrates most heavily on.

Jimmy says that wading is available too but the footing can be tough in the spring so make sure you have a wading belt and studs on your boots. I talk about my fabled "Green Rock Flop" elsewhere in the book, but if you are not as clumsy as I am, try it.

20 — HOUSATONIC RIVER

Now that I just finished the toughest river to write about because the Connecticut covers so much water and offers such fine fishing, let's get right into yet another extremely complex water, the Housatonic, and after you read this part, I hope you will walk away with some valuable information.

The river starts up at Pittsfield, Ma., and drops into the Sound 134 miles to the south. The main stem part that is in our state runs for 71 miles from the state line and its estuary covers another 13 miles. Because it is a combination of fresh, brackish, and salt, we have it in this chapter.

The main stem is hooked into by the Ten Mile, Still, Shepaug and Pomperaug rivers and stops at the Derby Dam. In our lake chapter we talk at length about two of the lakes that make up part of the 71 miles — Lillinonah and Zoar.

An old fact sheet about the river I got from the folks at Litchfield County also told me that there are four hydropower dams on the main stem — at the Falls Village Dam, The Bulls Bridge Dam, the Shepaug Dam which forms Lillinonah, and the Stevenson Dam which forms Zoar. The Derby Dam goes back to the 19th century and was built for waterpower for the mills of the day.

The 20-mile section from Falls Village to Kent is known for its fishing and offers excellent opportunity to folks who like to float fish via canoes or kayaks. A nine mile section in Cornwall and Sharon form the Trout Management Area that is strictly "catch and release."

The TMA runs from the bridge at Route 12 and 7 downstream to the bridge at Routes 4 and 7. From 6/15 through 8/31, those portions within 100 hundred feet of the mouths of tributary streams (shown on posters) are closed! At all other times, there is no "Closed Season," but it's fly only and, once again, "catch and release" only, period!

TIP: Brown trout to 22 inches or better are found in these waters and for the biggest kind try a March brown (what else for a "brownie"?) when the water flow is fast. Mid-afternoon is one time to try along with the more traditional early or late.

The Atlas tells us that the river has large and smallmouth bass along with trout. In addition, carp, eels, northern pike, and sunnies are in the freshwater sections. The Angler's Guide includes white catfish and white perch too, plus lots of yellow perch. And since it drops into the Sound south of the I95 Bridge in Stratford, it has the whole gamut of salt species too.

A fine boat launch may be found at Indian Well State Park at the north end of Shelton. It's open from 5/15 through 11/1, and speeding near shore is restricted.

Note: The Merritt Parkway crossing at Stratford/

Milford is the place where you are required to start carrying your freshwater license, NOT at the I95 bridge way to the south!!

Let's review some more things about the river now. You can start your year in February if you dress warm enough, at the Devon Power Plant where stripers are active. If you can find some of the gizzard shad that often are on top, catch one and use it for bait.

Spring fishing includes spinner flies and Hendrickson's working for trout and down below the trout water at the Devon Power Plant Discharge, stripers start getting more serious in the warm water. Flounder begin to feed near the mouth then and as the river warms, stripers spread around and are on the move.

Trout are after sulphur's and BWO's (Blue-winged olives) at the TMA, and in high water, go after caddis flies too. Late in June you might want to use a little #22 Needhami. Remember that tributary mouths are closed so keep away from them and catch your summer trout on streamers instead of little flies.

You can find a Bass Management Area between Dawn Hill Road, Sharon, and Skiff Mt. Road, Kent, and it has a six fish, no size limit rule for keeping black bass. This area is called "The Stanley Tract." Super smallie and very good largemouth action can be found here in the summer and at the Bulls Bridge bypass channel.

The flounder season ends and the fluke season starts in June with the toothy family members being caught in the lower river and this gets very good in July!

Stripers and fluke continue to feed in July down river, as the trout above are feeding on cream spinners and cahills in size 14, with white flies in cool early mornings. Next come Hickory shad and if you get a few, freeze them for catfish food. They make wonderful bait in chunks.

A white Wulff in size 12 is good in August at the TMA and the bronzeback action remains excellent at the Stanley Tract. The lower river continues to offer fluke and striped bass but try to fish when the tide isn't cranking.

As summer comes near its end the fluke leave the river, but you can catch plenty of trout up above on grasshopper look-alikes. A beetle imitation will work equally well.

My Coastal Access Guide Map (GET ONE) shows lots of places to get into the water. Running downstream, they include:

The Sunnyside Boat Ramp at Shelton, and then open water fishing from shore at South Bank off of Route 110, a little to the south of Sunnyside. Remember that these are spots that demand a freshwater license. Another spot is Caswell Cove on its east side. Then near the I95 Bridge is The Dock Shopping Center halfway down Stratford, which offers a variety of fishing opportunities. Further into the mouth on the west side is Bond's Dock where you can fish from shore and still find a toilet! Lastly, and what might be your best all-around site is the Birdseye Street Boat Launch which has just about everything — ramp, shore, etc.

21 — MIANUS RIVER

The river forms a big upside down U in Westchester County, N.Y., before dropping into the Mianus Reservoir, which touches both New York and Connecticut. The river starts again in Fairfield County.

It certainly doesn't compare in either size or quality of fishing to either of the two previous waters, but since the Connecticut and Housatonic are so special, let's just call this river a very good one instead.

What makes it very good is the fact that, although it's a river that is modest in size compared to the big guys, it has its own Trout Management Area that has good fishing.

This TMA is in Stamford, from Merribrook Road to the dam a mile or so upstream, and is so indicated by posters. From 3/1 to the third Saturday in April yearly, you may fish, but only with a single hook artificial lure only, and everything must be immediately released.

At all other times of the year you are allowed to catch and keep as many as three trout, which have to be at least nine inches long.

TIP: A good number of Seeforellen browns have been stocked here and all were under the nine-inch size limit. The hopes are for them to run out to sea and come back as adults. Therefore, if you catch a really small fish, don't get mad, just put it back carefully and hope that you see it on its return trip. They grow big and fast!

Including the Seeforellens, 3,430 is a typical year's stocking in the TMA, most of which are browns. The portion that is not TMA water, in Greenwich/Stamford, got 1,820 trout and here most were rainbows, with 30 breeders too.

Since the river runs out to sea, please note that you don't need a freshwater license once you get south of the dam on Boston Post Road in Greenwich.

I'm sorry to say that I couldn't find any access sites near the mouth of the river, which has nicely protected waters nearby in Cos Cob Harbor as well as around in Greenwich Cove a bit to the east.

22 — MYSTIC RIVER

While the Mianus has little to offer in the way of comfort to saltwater anglers, the Mystic is very angler-friendly.

Since just about the whole river is found in and around Mystic, if you can find that town, you can also find the river that wears its name. Mystic is at exit 90 off of I95 where a freshwater license is needed to the north of 95, down to 500 feet before you reach Route 1.

Shaffer's Boat Livery is right on the river and offers all kinds of bait and tackle, as well as rental boats.

I talked to fellow writer Bob Sampson who helped me out with some technical material about the river. I was having difficulty trying to find out about the freshwater population because most of the river's area demands such a license, but the truth is that it has little such life.

Bob told me that the river is started at Whitfords Brook, which itself is fed from Long Pond, another of our "75." Whitfords is at Ledyard/Stonington, and got 690 trout in a recent year and is generally on the state stocking list. While some trout might make it down into the Mystic, the only sweetwater fish that he has heard of were American and Hickory shad, so let's talk mostly about salt.

There are at least eight access sites on the river, including next to the old Sirtex Factory in the upper river. You can park at the right of way and walk out through the marsh. On the Stonington side of the brackish section you can launch at Isham Street. In downtown Mystic, you can park on the street next to the river park. There are three railroad bridge spots — at the Mystic River RR Bridge, the Willow Point RR Bridge and the Beebee Cove North RR Bridge. For each of the three, you can park at the W. Mystic P. O. Several others include Fort Rachel Marine for shore fishing, and the dock and launch site at Water Street.

TIP: The drawbridge at Route 1 is a very popular spot where anything from shad to flounder to fluke to blues to stripers can all be caught at one time or another. If you have time during the week, when it is a bit quiet, this is probably the best spot on the whole river.

Depending on the need to make a comeback, if and when they return in numbers, expect that winter flounder will be present in the lower river late each fall until they dig in for the winter. Once they pop out, the best style for them would involve using bank mussels as bait (the ones that are gray-shelled, not black, and contain yellow not orange meat). Make sure it is legal to dig them, if that is your choice, because many places are off limits. The best way to get them would be from your tackle store.

Fluke are a better bet at and outside of the mouth of the river, especially over towards the Groton Long Point area.

If you look at a map that gives you a close-up of the river, you will see that the harbor offers lees from virtually every direction of wind other than killer velocity. Shoreline protects you in the harbor from the north, west and east, and to the south, Mason Island offers you further lee.

Striped bass enter the river in substantial numbers, chasing small shad and eating anything else that gets in their way. While bluefish are not as common they too are here in the summer.

For certain, if you want to target a specific fish though, the number one occupant of the Mystic River by far is the summer flounder, the one we northerners call "fluke."

If you really, really, really are hung up on freshwater fish though, you can find lots of them and not even get worm gook on your hands. I highly recommend a visit to the Mystic Aquarium (1-860-572-5955). They are open nearly every day from 9-6. Check out the seals as you come in and the spectacularly colored Japanese Koi (carp family). Once inside, most sweetwater fish, as well as lots of salt lovers, can be viewed. No, not "fishin'," but fun anyway.

Captain David Orlowski (1-860-228-1483) runs two boats out of Noank and his smaller outfit is perfect for the river. From one hour before sunset until dark is when he looks for birds right in the mouth of the river to signal the presence of stripers and blues. He uses a small Kastmaster jig on a spinning outfit with 8-15 pound mono. At times he will switch to a fly rod with small white bucktail. In addition to the blues and striped bass, at times the water will be covered with more hickory shad then anything else.

23 — NIANTIC RIVER

Count on this one having no real "sweetwater" fish either, because only the tiniest part of the Niantic even calls for a freshwater license. It is that little piece that is north of that Golden Spur Bridge over Route 1. East Lyme is on the west side and Waterford is to the east of the bridge.

Since I felt a need to include every "Best" river that has some freshwater I put this one here, but truth be known, it really belongs in the Saltwater chapter!

While the DEP doesn't put any fish in, tides and current and just plain mother nature does, and they all start out and end up in salt-water.

Since white perch are by nature lovers of brackish water, about the only place that I can guess may have them in numbers would be above Route 1 in Banning Cove but don't make a special trip to try it out, please.

Instead, look for the wonderful population of fluke that come into the river each June. Fair to good striped bass action can be found in July in the river, with far better fluke catches. And if you want some feisty little Hickory shad, try for them early or late in the day.

Kayla Morgan Boyd and Capt. Arnie Costello with hickory shad caught in Niantic River.

TIP: Did you ever try herring strips for fluke bait? They work great. For this river, use shad strips instead. It is tough to fillet and strip frozen ones because of their bony structure. Therefore, if you catch some hickory's, take them home, and fillet them. Freeze the fillets skin to skin and when you take them out to use as bait, it will be pretty easy then to cut your strips. You may want to fillet away the thicker meat before freezing.

A sizable number of blue claw crabs pop up in the river each summer and here's an extra tip for you — When you want to eat crabs, do it all alone. If the kids or your significant other is present, they will beg or steal the best hunks for themselves without even saying so much as thank you!

Kidding aside, here again, use the shad as bait in your trap or on your hand line. A whole head works on the hand line but a whole fish itself is best in the trap.

The Route 156 railroad bridge separates the Niantic River from Niantic Bay (another of our "Best Waters"). A few access spots in the river are:

East Lyme
- the Grand Street Boat Launch on the west side
- the Niantic River Walkway (with handicap access and plenty of fishing room from land)
- Peninsula Park (where you can put a car-topper in and fish from land too)

Waterford Side
- The Niantic River State Boat Launch (with amenities galore — dock, shore, ramp, etc.)
- Capt. John's boats off of Second Street for a fun day on the water
- Sandy Point, well up river. Two sections of the river join here.

24 — THAMES RIVER

There are far and away many more access sites found on the Thames then on any of the other brackish to salt river that I will be writing about and a very serious potential problem can present itself with ease to you. The good part is that I have never experienced the problem, maybe because the badge wearers are very merciful here, but it may also be because I was just plain lucky!

You see, I fished the Thames with my son-in law Greg Morea and my grandchildren, Joe and Rebecca (they live nearby) many times before I found out that I needed a license!

The cut off point for a license is at Groton/New London, 500 feet north of Route 1! So, other than the one time that I went to the new pier on the western side of the river, every prior outing was not a legal one!

This river is often frequented by sailors stationed at the Sub Base. Connecticut offers a break to members of the armed forces who are not technically residents of the state. They only have to pay the same thing as a regular resident would fork out for a freshwater license. But the bottom line is that these sailors do need a license. My guess is that the ticket writers show mercy, but again, it is the law, so if you are "up river," you may be caught without a paddle and get ticketed if you don't have the necessary license.

The Thames is formed at the juncture of the Yantic (west) and Shetuckct (east) rivers, at Chelsea/Norwich Harbor.

I couldn't find a launch site one on my Atlas all the way down river from where it starts until you get to the Route I95 bridge. Two are here, one on the northeast side and the other on the southwest. But my superb copy of the Connecticut Coastal Access Guide showed me lots more! In fact, a friend with the DEP sent me a list that shows a total of 13 access sites in all.

Northernmost is the Poquetanuck Cove Boat Launch, Take Drawbridge Road immediately south of the Route 12 bridge. This site as well as the next one at Stoddard Hill State Park (High tide use only) is car-top only so be careful. A legitimate ramp and dock is the Town Boat Launch at Montville on the west side. Take Dock Road in Uncasville. Don't tie-off at the dock — not only is it impolite to others, it is also not allowed.

The city pier is new and is on the west side, south of Route I95. It's at the foot of State Street in New London, and offers plenty of handicap access and lots of fishing room, with fine lighting and seating — and rod holders tipped towards the water, a wonderful feature.

Across the river at Groton is the Ken Streeter State Boat Launch Site. It's off Fairview Avenue.

If you take Route 12 up along the river, driving slowly, you will see quite a few rustic parking areas, where folks simply pull up and park, then walk down the bank to the river. A train track needs to be crossed to reach the rocks. I guess I have fished this general area a dozen times and have never seen a train. Of course if one ever comes, you had better make for points elsewhere.

TIP: Fishing from shore can be very good or very bad, depending on the fancy of the fish. When the water warms up, bluefish and stripers go on their feed and the best bait, by far, is a simple chunk of mackerel. While seaworms or clams work, just buy a whole mackerel and cut off little pieces. The part that runs along the lateral line is best. It is a combination of oily, colorful, and bright. Don't cut chunks with bones on — leave the skeleton intact. A 1½ inch by 1½ inch square, hooked twice with a size 1/0 hook is what you want. Stand the pole up between rocks, tighten the line, and open the drag — and now just sit back and wait 'em out. They will come!

Way up at the Poquetanuck Cove launch site talked about above can be found some nice white perch fishing around the end of April, but since stripers and blues are the main goal in the river, let's talk about them.

Farther up river than this site, not far from where it starts, is super striped bass fishing early each season. Norwich Harbor is the site, and live alewives, if you can buy them, are the top bait for the biggest linesides. Schoolies can be caught here from your boat with flies. Try the flashiest streamer you can find to match the "sawbellies."

The striped bass bite continues up near Norwich for most of the spring but as the water warms further, the big guys leave and are replaced by their offspring.

Stripers remain on station in good numbers from the Montville Power Plant up to Norwich later in the spring and some flounder have popped up too out of hibernation.

Winter flounder are spread throughout the river from the Power Plant on down to the mouth of the river each spring but, unless they make a wonderful recovery and spawn in good numbers again, don't count on too many fillets.

Bluefish get into the river near the summer and mix with the bass. We don't recommend using wire because you will get more bites without it, but a happy medium would be the use of a long shank hook after you get bit off a time or two.

Some autumn action with flounder starts up as they return to the river, and at the same time, charging schools of false albacore and bonito appear at the mouth of the river. The blues leave late in the fall but stripers remain on station.

And oh yes, just outside of the mouth of the river itself, if you know the area, own a Loran, have a good bottom reading machine AND someone gave you his "numbers," you might stick an anchor overboard. Larry Krizen did that in November of 2000 and plopped an 8.5 pound blackfish onto the deck!

HONORABLE MENTION

- The **TMA on the Hammonasset River at Killingworth —** Madison is a good stretch. Look it up in your Anglers Guide.
- **The Mill River** just missed the cut-off. It runs out into Southport Harbor, but the area worth discussing is the TMA in Fairfield from the Merritt down to Lake Mohegan.
- **The Pawcatuck River** — right alongside the R.I. line.
- **The Saugatuck River** runs out between Norwalk and Westport.
- **The Tankerhoosen River — Vernon —** has the Belding WILD TMA — !

CHAPTER 3

Freshwater Rivers

25 — FARMINGTON RIVER

B ack in 1994, the West Branch of the Farmington River became the first river in the state, and actually, the fourth in the whole country, to become classified as a national Wild and Scenic River. This 14 mile stretch of the river thus received the strongest river protection available in the entire country from any federally funded or permitted project that might have any direct adverse effect on the river.

The river begins as the "West Branch" below Hogback Dam, where West Branch Reservoir (Hogback) ends. This is in Hartford County, a bit below the border with Massachusetts, and between the towns of Colebrook and Hartland. It flows on down to the town of Riverton.

The middle section of the Farmington River starts in Riverton, and the Still River, ending in the town of Farmington, 25 miles downstream joins it. Both of these stretches are famous for the huge number of trout that they contain. The portion between the Route 4 bridge in Unionville and the Route 4 bridge (River Road) in Farmington offers fine canoe fishing for trout as well as yellow perch and crappie.

When you reach the lower section on your map, you will see

*We got this snap of a fine Farmington brownie from Grady Allen
at UpCountry Sportfishing (1-800-379-1952).*

that the river forms a big U in the northern section of the state,
finally turning east at Tariffville from where it flows out into the
Connecticut River.

The top and middle sections are best known for their trout
populations, and because the water heats up in its lowest part, we
get into some wonderful warm water action.

Some special rules that I found to apply to the river are:

- The part of the West Branch that flows at Barkhamsted —
New Hartford from about a mile upstream of the Route 318
Bridge is restricted to barbless hooks downstream to the
Route 219 Bridge. Signs indicate this too. This whole stretch
is "catch and release" only — possession of trout here is
strictly prohibited.

- The section that runs from Avon to Burlington, from the base
of the LOWER Collinsville Dam downstream for three miles
to the Route 4 Bridge has no closed season for trout but from
3/1 to Opening Day, every trout you catch must be safely

This fat rainbow trout was taken on a fly by Maria Rose Boyd in the Farmington River.

released. During the open season you may keep as many as five and they have to be at least 9 inches long.

As you get further south, at Windsor, from the mouth of the tailrace canal, below Rainbow Dam, downstream to where it enters the Connecticut River, very special regulations apply to a variety of fish. I suggest you consult with the most important (Well, maybe second most because I'd like to think this book is the "MOST" important) piece of reading material you can have, the Anglers Guide, to check what rules apply to your style of fishing.

In addition to the large number of fish the state stocks in the river, The Farmington River Anglers Association distributes as many as one thousand large trout annually in the "catch and release" area towards the end of the spring.

The 99/00 stocking records I saw showed that the area of the river in Hartford County got 14,170 trout from the state and the larger sections in Litchfield County received 35,125. 260 of these were particularly large fish.

And if that impresses you, let's look at the attempts made by Connecticut to establish an Atlantic Salmon fishery in the river. Including those fish stocked through the entire three sections, a grand total of 814,358 fry were put in! Another 31,040 fingerling-sized salmon were added also.

When the river is high, releases from Hogback into the West Branch can be slowed to help maintain flood control.

TIP: Consider using a blue-winged olive at the start of May for some of the biggest kind of holdover brownies.

Hendrickson's are a good fly in the spring, as are a tan or green caddis. In mid-May of 2000, Ray Vincent caught a 7.3 pound brownie. And a month later, Patrick McNamara had a 5.11 brownie.

Go with sizes 18-20 caddis or little #26-28 B. W. O.'s early or late in the day as it warms up more.

A wide assortment of flies will attract trout, including the above variety but also try a dark bead head nymph in size 16, and bigger Isonychia's — up to #12. Come summer a #24 chocolate Needhami is an idea late each day. The warmer the air, the better you can do with a wide assortment, like terrestrials, and even streamers.

Down below a bit, the shad fishing heats up for a week or two and for them, my friend Charlie Zaimes says you should use a lot of different color of darts or spoons, providing they are red and white, red and white, or red and white.

The lower river has super smallie action. For example, Jeffrey Paine nailed a 4.15 bronzeback monster in June 2000.

Channel catfish are plentiful at the mouth of the river, with Portland to Haddam best. And for another huge fish that many an angler wants to hook up, how about carp to 20 pounds on corn kernel? In addition, northern pike too. Largemouth bass, sunfish and eels are present as well.

Aside from the Connecticut and the Housatonic Rivers, we won't have as many details about other rivers in the state for you, but clearly, the Farmington warrants the space.

26 — MOOSUP RIVER

The Moosup River Trout Management Area has some very big brown trout. But two huge rainbows were caught in the river in the spring of 2000 also. A 9-pounder was reported late in May and earlier in the month, Jerry Simonds caught one that was an ounce under 8 pounds.

The river is just west of the Rhode Island line, and canoe lovers put in here at Fairbanks Corner. They also enter at the Almyville Dam, Brunswick Avenue off Goshen Road, off Route 14. Its TMA is in Plainfield, from the Route 14 bridge at the treatment plant downstream to the junction with the Quinebaug River. This stretch is fly only and every trout caught must be immediately returned to the water alive.

TIP: There is no closed season here, so you can fish for fun the year 'round, but remember, put them all back.

The TMA part got 2,225 fish in the 1999/2000 season, including a handful of brookies. Most were brown trout and 25 of those were called Special Breeder Size. The river is open from Plainfield/ Sterling and 3,380 trout went in the open section one year, most of which were rainbows. 40 big breeder browns were stocked too. The river runs past a series of dams and covers 23 miles.

27 — NATCHAUG RIVER

Look for this river at Chaplin — Eastford — Windham and expect some pretty scenery with fine early season trout action. An easy Trout Park is here as well.

Access sites can be intermittently found from Route 198 to Route 6., not far from Mansfield Hollow Lake a bit to the west.

If you want to try a canoe drift trip for trout, less experienced boaters can float the least dangerous stretch from just south of the junction of Route 198 and 44 in Phoenixville, off General Lyons Road. A seven-mile run takes you through pretty flat water, with some quick stuff too, past several dams and bridges to England Road bridge.

One of the largest stockings of brook trout in the state went here, 3,080 of them one year. 80 big breeder rainbows were also stocked among the 9,940 'bows, and 6,590 browns went in. So while I don't have too much to tell you about the river other than where it is and what's in it, suffice it to say that with so many fish stocked annually, you might want to give it a shot.

TIP: For waders who like to dunk bait, the best bait by far over the last several years will certainly work here. I'm talking about the shrimp flavored pink salmon egg. In case you don't want to take your catch home though, please clamp down the barb on your hook and cut your line if the fish swallowed it.

Fall stockings might include little surplus yearling browns and rainbows so in particular, for these fish, handle with care and put them back, okay?

While trout are the main goal here, like the 4½ pound rainbow that Scotty Barnes caught in the spring of 2000, eight-year young Brady Guay nailed a huge smallmouth bass in the river. It weighed 4.1 pounds!

28 — NAUGATUCK RIVER

The West and East Branches of the Naugatuck River join in Torrington, and flow south as the main body, and from the juncture down to the Thomaston Flood Control Dam, some fine trout fishing can be had, with a bonus too!

Much of the river can be found at or very near to Route 8. The west branch is stocked from Stillwater Pond to Route 4. The east branch receives fish from the Meyer Road Bridge for 2,000 feet along Newfield Road.

The bonus discussed above is Atlantic Salmon. 3-10 pound broodstock salmon are stocked during October, November and December. The two spots are:

1. from the Route 118 bridge crossing in Litchfield downstream to the Thomaston Flood Control Dam
2. from the Union City Dam (Naugetuck) downstream to the Tingue Dam (Seymore). 616 of these big fish went in one recent year.

Special regulations pertain here to salmon, and you can bet that they might change too. Don't count on it always being this way, but for some time it said that the season was open from the third Saturday in April clear through the end of March. A single hook, on a lure or otherwise, is the only style permitted, with no separate weight added. The creel limit is one salmon per day.

TIP: Try a weighted body woolly bugger on a floating line.

Beacon Falls and Campville are good places to try for an Atlantic. Alternate flies would be a size 6 or 8 gray ghost or a Mickey Finn streamer.

The area of the main branch at Harwinton and Litchfield got 54,861 trout one year, 40 of which were breeder rainbows. A handful of other 'bows and some brookies were put in too, but the overwhelming majority were brown trout. The east and west branches received another 2,610 trout.

So if you are after trout, the river has lots of them. But you might also be surprised to see an Atlantic salmon come rocketing out of the water with your fly. It is up to you of course, but a careful release might please you as much as it would the fish and other anglers as well.

29 — PACHAUG RIVER

A very fine Waters Guide I received from the folks at "Connecticut's Quiet Corner" — Box 598, Putnam, C.T. 06260, told me a little about this river, found in their northeast corner of the state. The brochure provides a lot of useful material about many of the lakes and rivers in their area and I suggest you write for a copy.

We will discuss Pachaug Pond in Griswold later in the book. For now, let's talk about the river. A portion of the river can be found west of Pachaug Pond at Griswold and then it appears again to the east near Voluntown where it is at Beach Pond (also described in the lake portion) right near the Rhode Island line. Route 138 E/W will take you near the river at both ends. Sections of the river are stocked from Beach Pond on back west to the Quinebaug River.

A normal trout stocking would include some breeder rainbows as part of 4,810 fish overall. Some would be brookies and others brown trout, but most are rainbows, making up 60+% of the total number.

TIP: Pachaug holds a substantial population of bass, in addition to its trout. Try for your bass with a clean (no hair or other fuzzies) #2 or #3 Mepps spinner. Since a #3 is heavier, let the current of the day determine which you use — #2 in light current, #3 in stronger. If the day is clear, use silver. On a dark day go with a gold lure.

Fishing access is available for disabled persons at the boat launch on Beachdale Pond (halfway between Pachaug and Beach Ponds) off Route 49 North.

Spring or fall, trout or bass, fish Pachaug.

30 — SALMON RIVER

We won't be talking about "Salmon Brook" here, but you can certainly consider it as an "Honorable Mention" site. The Brook can be found in and around Granby and it usually receives 11,000+ trout each year. It also got a large number of Atlantic Salmon fry in recent years too.

Our subject now, however, is the Salmon River, and while salmon certainly have been put into the river, the primary target is trout, so let's talk about that for a while now.

This site is a little tricky, because one map I have says it dumps into the Connecticut River at the Haddam Neck Wildlife

Management Area, and another (the one put out by our friends at the DEP), shows that it joins the Moodus River before the Moodus hooks up with the Connecticut. So whether it is a direct or indirect connection, you know that the river eventually winds up joining the Connecticut River.

The river runs through Colchester, E. Haddam, E. Hampton, and Haddam, with fishing from the junction with the Blackledge River down to the Leesville Dam.

A special Trout Management Area is in Colchester, from the junction with the Blackledge and Jeremy Rivers on down to the Old Browns Mill Dam. Posters in this area show that it is fly fishing only. There is no closed season either, and from the third Saturday in April through the last day in August you are allowed to keep five trout if they are at least nine inches long. From 9/1 on until Opening Day comes around again, this water is strictly "catch and release!" That means zero can be kept, — or detained.

TIP: The regulation says that all trout must be "immediately returned, without avoidable injury." To me, that also means "NO POSING FOR PICTURES OR MEASURING OR WEIGHING." I don't know how strictly the state enforces rules, but the words tell me that you can get a summons if you do anything else but IMMEDIATE release. Understand?

The TMA offers beautiful scenery and an easy access Trout Park, with weekly stockings occurring through May.

9,760 trout is a typical year's TMA stocking. Some are brook trout while many are browns. More still are rainbow trout with a bunch of breeder 'bows added yearly. As you move from New London County down into Middlesex County and closer to the joint with the Connecticut, yet another group of nearly 11,000 trout is added here. 80+% are rainbows.

The list of "Top Spots" that I got from the State said that the area of the lower river around E. Haddam/Haddam, above the Cove, offers just about every kind of fish that you can find in the state. Remember, the river hooks up with the Connecticut, so a variety of fish can and will visit upstream from time to time.

They include but are not limited to some shad and herring each spring, plus pickerel and pike, yellow and white perch, all the catfish that the state has, rock and calico bass, large and small-mouth bass, sunfish, plus wandering stripers, and salmon too.

Salmon? Well, 98,213 fry were stocked throughout the river over a recent two-year period so, hopefully, many of them wound up heading out the Connecticut and will return as adults to the Salmon River when they mature.

31 — SHETUCKET RIVER

Atlantic Salmon broodstock have been dropped into the river and since it is unlikely that most anglers in the state have much access to salmonoids that go from 3-10 pounds elsewhere, let's get you to this river now!

Situated in the eastern part of the state, the river is formed at the confluence of the Willimantic and Natchaug Rivers. It then joins the Quinebaug River near Taft Station. Controlled water releases come from the Mansfield Dam, or else the river gets too shallow at times.

The best salmon fishing comes from the areas the fish are stocked at each autumn. They are between the Scotland Dam in Scotland, and in Norwich, at the Occum Dam. The very best fishing can be found upstream of the Route 57 bridge in Baltic.

Canoe lovers can enter at the Greenville Dam Recreation Area in Norwich. Besides salmon, trout and bass are caught with regularity in this area by folks who are drift/fly fishing.

The salmon season is open from Opening Day in April clear through March 31st and as elsewhere, you can only catch them on a single free-swinging hook, by itself or as part of a lure, to avoid the horrors that used to occur with regularity up north in the rivers that join with Lake Ontario — SNAGGING!). You may keep one per day.

TIP: Try a muddler minnow. They are one of the best salmon attractors around.

As with the Naugatuck River, 616 special breeder sized salmon went into the Saugatuck in the fall of 1999.

The northern section in Windham County received 500 browns one year but down below in New London County, 4,760 mixed

*Ron Whiteley fishes all over the world but he caught this fine
8 pound Atlantic salmon in the Shetucket River.*

brown and rainbow went in from Sprague on down. Much of this
water is found directly off of Route 97.

Because the Shetucket hooks up with the Quinebaug and they
then enter the Thames, which of course drops into the Sound, a substantial number of shad travel northward to spawn in the Shetucket
some years. The end of April is the best time to try for shad and the
Greenville Dam may be the top spot in the river for them.

Smallies are other fish that are taken in the river.

32 — WILLIMANTIC RIVER

Brown trout are the main game here, and the river offers fine
fishing for them. The best known area is called the "Cole Wilde

Trout Management Area" and let's go to it.

Look for the river near Coventry, Mansfield, Tolland and Willington. Route 32 or Route 6 are the nearest roads to the river.

The TMA starts at the mouth of Roaring Brook on down to the bridge at Route 74 and these waters are open year round to fly fishing only and it is "catch and release" only. No doubt this is an area that the good guys at Trout Unlimited fish often for just that reason.

A typical stocking at the TMA involved 1,825 fish. 25 were big brownies and another 1,300 9-12 inchers went in. 500 rainbow trout also are stocked in the Cole Wilde waters.

The open waters in this area get 5,210 trout, including more rainbow then brown, and some of the rainbows are broodstock beasts. Below the TMA in Stafford, yet another 2,100 trout go in and in two consecutive years, 40 breeder browns were included in that number. All these are in Tolland County and in Windham County, 2,060 more trout were added to the river.

TIP: If you are a sissy like me and don't like to show off your "Green Rock Flop" skills as I do whenever I wade, trout can be caught from shore too. Cast straight ahead of you, and whether it is a lure or bait, be particularly ready for a bite as your hook starts to rise from the bottom. Look at your watch now — if you are fishing downstream from left to right, 90% of your strikes will come as the hook is at 2 o'clock or so. Fishing from right to left, the rise and strikes will take place at 10 o'clock. I'm sorry if many of you know this already, but if a handful of you learned something, I'm glad about it.

HONORABLE MENTION

There's a ton of small streams and rivers shown in the Guide. One good one would be Bladdens Brook's TMA in Seymour. Another is the Salmon Brook in Granby. But there are really so many others that I suggest you find one shown in the Guide that is near your home and enjoy its relative quiet and good fishing.

CHAPTER 4

Lakes / Ponds / Reservoirs

33 — AMOS LAKE

L ocated in Preston, this lake is best known for its quality pickerel and largemouth bass. It is a "Trophy Trout" lake, one that is subject to special regulations.

Generally speaking, Trophy Trout Lakes such as Amos are closed from 3/31 until the third Saturday in April.

TIP: But at Amos Lake, any trout that you want to take home in March itself must measure at least 16 inches, and your daily creel limit is two.

A typical stocking year at Amos involved a grand total of 10,040 trout put in, including a handful of brookies. About ¼ were brown trout and the rest rainbows. So, while we call this a venue best known for its largemouth bass and pickerel, remember too that it holds lots of trout!

To reach Amos Lake from Norwich, the closest large city, travel east on Route 165 until you get to Route 164 and then south on 164 for 1½ miles and then go right (east) on a narrow road to the lake. A boat ramp exists on its western side, about halfway down its shoreline.

In order to accommodate anglers and other boaters alike, special rules apply regarding boating. You cannot operate a boat faster than

8 mph here, except for the period between 6/15 to the first Sunday after Labor Day. During those warm weeks, between the hours of 11 a.m. and 6 p.m., water skiers and other boaters may push the power up.

So if you are an early riser in the summer, or like to fish late, hold your speed. It's not only the right thing to do... it is also the law!

Amos Lake contains 112 acres, and reaches a maximum depth of 48 feet straight out from the ramp in the middle. A good portion is 42 feet deep when full, and a substantial portion of the top section of the lake is 36 feet deep.

Holdover brown trout are taken in its deepest waters early each season, and this continues until late Spring.

Largemouth bass take over as summer approaches, but do remember that if you want to take a few home for a meal, they must reach at least a foot in length.

Amos Lake holds a substantial number of large bluegills, and since this fish is a crowd-pleaser, don't forget to bring a kid with you to this fine lake.

The boat ramp is concrete plank, a fine one, but it gets crowded. The parking area can accommodate approximately 20 vehicles with trailers.

We have already told you that the lake contains bluegills, trout, bass and pickerel. Add to that list yellow perch, bullhead and eel and that makes up its main occupants.

34 — BALL POND

Do you like quiet? The regulations at Ball Bond forbid the use of engines, PERIOD! The lake covers nearly 90 acres, and has depths ranging down to 45+ feet. It offers adequate parking and good fishing. The ramp area is shallow so be careful to launch with caution.

TIP: Remember, You cannot even have a lifted engine on your boat! NO MOTORS, gas or electric, okay?

The lake can be found west of New Fairfield, a short distance east of the New York line. Route 39 goes around its western side

I had to get my mug in my own book! Here I am with a good sized pike, typical of what you can catch at Bantam Lake.

and the boat ramp can be found at its southern edge.

The waters closest to the ramp are quite shallow, with the deep water found way up towards the northern third.

Most of the trout that the state stocks here are brownies, with 5,000+ browns and rainbows overall put in yearly.

Besides trout, the resident population includes lots of large-mouth bass. Summer to late fall is the best time to catch them, but since fall stockings of trout are common, you may catch both in good numbers that time of year.

Brown bullhead and sunnies round out the balance of fish.

The lake closes to fishing the last day in February and reopens again at 6:00 a.m. on the third Saturday in April for trout lovers.

35 — BANTAM LAKE

Northern pike, (1,074 more were stocked in 1999/2000), small and largemouth bass, yellow and white perch, plus crappie and catfish live in this lake, situated at Morris/Litchfield. Now if that doesn't get your juices going, you better take up bowling!

While @#%water skiing+!" is allowed here, the state has a law in place which permits us fishermen to have at least a degree of comfort as they go 'round and 'round. You see, other than during take-off or landing, these boats are not allowed within 150 feet of the shoreline.

My copy of the 2001 Connecticut Boater's Guide said that a fee is charged to use the boat ramp, which you can find way down in the southeast tip of the lake.

You can get to the lake from Route 202, Bantam, by heading south onto 209, but the preferred method to reach the boat ramp is via 109, turning north on East Shore Road.

TIP: During legal coldwater fishing times, try a style that Tony Broomer, an Englishman whom I met, taught to me for pike. He likes to use dead bait (and in particular, dead bait that floats) for pike. In shallow water, hook a smelt, shiner or herring under the lateral line, behind its refuse passageway. A two-foot leader is needed below your barrel swivel that is stopped by an egg sinker. Dropped to bottom, the dead bait will float up two feet to where the pike will think that it is a dying bait instead of a corpse. This works so you well that you will tell your friends that you invented the system!

While bass anglers often like to go after their prey in the dark, please realize that Bantam Lake forbids the use of motors from 11:00 p.m. to 5:00 a.m.!

Bantam is one of the most popular lakes in the state for northern pike. In order to help it maintain its popularity, the season closes for pike for all of March and April. This is the time that pike spawn. Since they get ready for this event during the other cold months, you are only allowed to keep one northern between December 1st and the end of February, and the fish must be at least 36 inches long. Of course we are not advocating taking any home at any time, but if that is your choice, make sure you follow the law, please.

Bantam is not a deep lake, 20+ feet deep at most in its 916 acres.

Live bait is far and away the best style for pike; slowly trolling it may be better at times than just watching a float. For trolling, hook your large shiner in the mouth and out an eyehole.

Bantam is a very popular lake for ice fishing with pike, largemouth bass, and yellow perch as the main targets. Jig for the perch, but the best style for bass and northerns is, of course, the time-tested tip-up with shiner. Just remember that from 12/1 through all of February, if you want to bring a pike home, it must be at least 36 inches.

If you can get out mid-week in the summer, you may escape the speed boaters. Of course they are normally on the water mid-day anyway. Since Wednesday is Doctor Day, you will have the best chance for quiet if you fish from 5 to 8 a.m., or 7 to 9 p.m., Monday, Tuesday, Thursday, and Friday.

Summer is a good time to catch smallies on deep running crayfish imitations. A little grub will produce some fine yellow perch and crappie catches too.

The lake contains lots of largemouth bass, and if you fish at night, bullheads come out to eat in large number on night crawlers.

36 — BASHAN LAKE

Bashan covers 276.3 acres, and is nearly 50 feet deep in the middle. Its feature players are trout, largemouth bass, yellow perch and sunnies. Other inhabitants are smallmouth bass, pickerel and calico bass (black crappie).

The ramp is found way down in the southern tip of the lake, and you can get to the lake in East Haddam by turning east off Route 82 onto Mt. Parnassus/Millington Road, and then left onto Ballahack Road, from where you travel 9/10 of a mile on a dirt road to the access area.

If you have the time to plan a two day trip, you may want to fish at Moodus Reservoir, just a little to the north of Bashan. We will discuss Moodus later in the book.

TIP: And use this one elsewhere too, of course. If you are looking for what I consider the very best live bait hook of all, it is a size 6, model 3906 Mustad, period! Yes, we talk about the more skinny wired Aberdeen model too, but I really like the 3906 (we used to call them "Sproat"). The rounded bend and strong steel is tops for me.

The number of catchable trout stocked into Bashan Lake varies from year to year. Over a recent four year period, for example, I discovered that 2,580 went in first, then 3,560, and the next two years, 2,820 were stocked. In all those years, many more rainbow trout were put in than brownies.

During the period between 9 p.m. and 8 a.m., your boat cannot operate at speeds in excess of 8 mph. At all other times, you may travel at 35 miles per hour (but not near me or get ear plugs to avoid my cussin'). Several other regulations exist regarding boating, but since we are here to talk fishing, we will omit such material.

Watch yourself when launching because the ramp is narrow and the channel is modest before you get into the lake itself. Remember to stay to the right to avoid conflict with boaters heading the other way.

You will find good numbers of largemouth bass in deeper water during the summer, and here a fish finder will come in handy because you should see submerged wood which is the best area of all to fish.

As you head out from the ramp, you will quickly be in 12 feet of water. However, close to the launch, you will read a gradual climb of depth from 12 to as little as 3 feet of water (nearly halfway across the first part of the lake from its right-hand shoreline). At this little submerged island, only a few feet below the surface, you will have to move quietly but in doing so, you may be rewarded by a powerful slam from a bass that is hiding.

The lake reaches down to nearly 50 feet deep in the middle, and if you want trout, often the best action from them is partially submerged over the deepest water you can find. They roam, and so should you.

37 — BEACH POND

This lake is in two states, so you must know about the regulations that prevail in Rhode Island as well as in Connecticut. Most of it is in New London County, but the eastern side lies in Washington County, Rhode Island. The closest town is Voluntown. Travel east from town on 138/165, and then when it splits, stay on 165. Swing north up Forge Hill Road and then right onto North Shore Road to the pay boat ramp, located on the north side of the lake. It's one of the lakes that offers handicap access.

Beach received 8,090 trout in a recent year from Connecticut, with more than 75% of them rainbows. And my guess is that Rhode Island adds plenty too. (If and when I do a Rhode Island book, I guess I will find out just how many).

TIP: Even though the main trout found is a 'bow, look for brownies in excess of two pounds hanging near bottom in the deepest water when the lake is either warmest or coldest. Try jigging a ¾ ounce Crippled Herring in dark blue and silver finish and remember that most hits on a jig come at the bottom of its downward trajectory.

There are times though in the summer when trout are caught in 15-20 feet of water while trolling small spoons.

You can fish anywhere on the lake if you hold a Connecticut or a Rhode Island license. Special regulations include the lake being closed on the last day in February. Bass rules say that a 12-inch limit prevails. And for pickerel, it is a 14-inch size limit. Trout don't have a size requirement, and you can only keep five of any kind.

Ice fishing is popular on Beach Pond and you may not use more than six tip-ups, but remember, no fishing once March 1st rolls around until Opening Day.

While 30-42 feet deep water can be found a short distance away from the ramp to the left, if you head further east towards the Rhode Island line you will find water that goes all the way down to 60 feet.

Known primarily for its trout fishing, don't discount the very fine fishing available at Beach Pond for largemouth bass. The "Green Grass Syndrome" applies here. (The Grass is greenest on the other side). Try for bass in the shallower water to the right of the ramp. A 6 mph speed limit exists at this end of the lake.

Other fish at Beach include smallies, pickerel, sunfish and yellow perch. Enjoy!

38 — BILLINGS LAKE

Another lake with handicap access is Billings. Here again, to allow the stocking trucks to roll and keep put and take anglers from removing trout right away, the lake is closed at the end of February to the 3rd Saturday in April.

Billings is in North Stonington, and while only 105 acres, holds a wide variety of fish. It is heavily fished for trout, but also has largemouth bass, pickerel, crappie, yellow perch, sunfish and bullhead.

To find the lake, (situated in a great area for other spots in this book like Pachaug Pond, Beach Pond and Wyassup Lake), travel Route 201 North from No. Stonington to Billings Road and hang a right to the lake where you will find the ramp nearby. The parking area is modest so I suggest hitting the road early to secure space.

A scattering of trout go into the lake, including brookies and browns, with more rainbows than both of them combined.

TIP: For put and take fishing early in the season, go with what the British call "Pop-Up" fishing. Use a pink or orange miniature marshmallow and then add a mealworm. Rig for casting from shore with a small egg sinker, and stop it with a barrel swivel, with your hook a foot or two away. The hook with 'mallow attached will lift off the bottom and "pop-up" and down in the water, waving the mealie where a waiting trout can find a little snack.

The boat ramp here is gravel, and the road leading to it is tough to drive so don't speed, please. Located a short distance away to the west is Anderson Pond/Blue Lake, so if you have time to check out another spot after you leave the ramp, just go back straight on Billings Lake Road to the access road to the other spot.

While you may not catch any trophy-sized holdover trout in Billings, a good opportunity exists for bass angling. The Atlas says that largemouth bass are commonly found, but the State's DEP Bulletin No. 10 (which was a great help to me, thanks, Lori, for the suggestion) says it holds smallies too. Pickerel, yellow perch, and sunfish are other fish that swim its waters.

18 feet of water is quickly reached straight out and to the southeast you will find its deep water, 30 feet.

An island pops up towards the lake's southern section, and quiet bass anglers can enjoy fine action while throwing dark rubber worms to shore.

39 — BOLTON LAKE, LOWER

I hope I don't give you a headache trying to find this place. You see, it has an alias, Willimantic Reservoir, and has a few brothers too like Upper Bolton, and Middle Bolton, both in Vernon. The lower section is in Bolton itself, and is the main target for this spot. (But don't omit the two other sections). A car top access is way at its north end and a regular ramp is nearby off Watch Hill Road. Its maximum depth is only 24 feet.

All three sections have 6 hp speed limits. At 178 acres, the lower lake is bigger than the other two parts and offers much more parking also.

To find the lower lake, take Route 44 and just west of the Quarryville Cemetery, head north to the boat ramp.

Not containing trout, the lake holds many another fish, including large and smallmouth bass, yellow perch, sunnies, chain pickerel, and brown bullhead.

The ramp here is very good but gets crowded with sailboats in the summer. As with other lakes we will tell you about, if you can avoid a summer weekend, do so. While I have tried to co-exist with "sailors," they do tend to tax your patience as they spend a half day rigging and re-rigging as you try to launch or leave the lake.

TIP: Have a spare rod handy, rigged with a single, large hook. Try to catch a little sunnie or perch and put it on the hook, live-lined. Cast it out, with no float or sinker, and let it swim. "Mr. Bucketmouth" bass may just visit. You will know it, and "Cross its eyes" with a mighty slam! ("catch and release" would be a nice idea).

40 — CANDLEWOOD LAKE

It's not an ocean, and certainly is not nearly as big as any of the Great Lakes, but Candlewood is far and away the largest lake in all of Connecticut at 5,420 acres. In fact, Candlewood is more than twice as large as any other lake in the Nutmeg State.

A little more than half of it sits in Fairfield County and to the east, the rest is in Litchfield County. The State stocked 41,480 trout in it between the summers of '99 and '00. Nearly 60% were brownies.

Pick a town in the two counties noted above and you could say that it is near Candlewood! (The best known are Danbury to the south and New Fairfield to the west).

At its juncture with Squantz Pond, halfway down along its western side, you may launch your boat. The spot is called Squantz Cove and is accessed via Squantz Pond State Park off Route 39, New Fairfield. Canoes are common there but please don't venture out into the open lake in one. It could be your last trip!

While there is room for 100+ vehicles here, the water level is often too low in drought conditions for a trailer so unless you are putting a car-topper in, you may want to call the park to find out if the ramp is usable at 1-203-797-4165.

Another launch site can be found way down in its southeast tip at Lattins Cove, Danbury, and here there also is room for 100+ vehicles with trailers. Again, call Squantz Park to make sure there is enough water at the ramp to launch.

TIP: In all three publications that I used for research, I found that the lake holds a wide variety of fish. But none talk about a critter that some value over all kinds. So, if you see a guy fishing from shore with two 10-12 foot rods, set just right on a fancy metal double forked stick, with electronic (HONEST) bite indicators attached to their lines, and they talk kind of funny, they are "Carpers." Candlewood Lake is home to countless carp, and these anglers are more often than not from England, where carp are far and away the most popular of all beasts.

So, what fish do the books I looked at talk about? Well for sure, bass galore are in Candlewood. Bucketmouths are just about everywhere. Many a tournament is held at Candlewood by most of the bass clubs in the state. Upwards of ten islands and peninsulas are in the lake, and if you cannot find a dock you like to throw plastics or spinner baits to, then fish off any points of land at these spots for a near-certain slam from a largemouth. As with carp, I couldn't find smallmouth in any of the publications but several of the weekly fishing reports put out by the State say that it has lots of bronzebacks too.

Trout hold over in the lake and as a result, it has special trophy trout regulations which, because they could change, I am not quoting. Suffice it to say that you should check out your rulebook before trying to catch and keep a trout. At last look, the lake is closed from 3/31 through Opening Day. For March, two trout could go home with you if they were at least 16 inches long.

To catch trout late in the spring, try trolling a spoon pretty quickly, 12-18 feet below the surface. You might get a rainbow that just went in a few weeks ago, or a football shaped holdover brown. Later yet, go deeper, as the top water gets too warm for trout. Just remember, bright lures are best.

In addition to carp, bass and trout, other occupants include bullhead and white catfish, white and yellow perch, crappie, pickerel and sunfish.

Don Loftus Jr. caught the state record white perch here in 1996. It pulled the de-liar down to 2.15 pounds. While not stocked in the lake any longer and not at all a commonly found species, the record walleye was taken 50+ years ago in 1941 by George Brita. It went 14½ pounds.

Trolling accounts for many of the fish caught and one reason may simply be that you cover more water that way. Another may be that if you try standing and casting during the day when the speed limit is, urph, 45 mph, you might get knocked out of the boat. By the way, no kidding, if he/she gets seasick, leave them home on a summer weekend.

Live bait works well for every fish, but if you have access to crawfish, find some rocks and fish for smallies. They love the critters called "Crabs" on Lake Ontario.

Just about all year long, something is available here, from pickerel on shiners early or late in the year, to white and yellow perch on fathead minnows or little grubs.

Boat rentals are available at Echo Bay Marina. They are bigger than the usual rental boats you see elsewhere, but that is because the lake demands such craft. Most are pontoon/deck boats and are quite sturdy. (1-203-775-7077).

This briefly summarizes what is available to anglers here. I might just sit down and write a separate book about Candlewood one day, as I have done about three other lakes but for now, let me just say: "Try it, you'll like it."

41 — COLEBROOK RESERVOIR

The reservoir is also called Colebrook River Lake or Colebrook Flood Control Impoundment, and its northernmost tip sticks up into Massachusetts. The lake is in Colebrook, Connecticut, mostly, and very little data is available about it.

Much of the lake's western side is available via Route 8 where the Army Corp. of Engineers has a boat ramp that may be unusable during periods of low water.

A 20 mph speed limit is in place on the lake and either a Connecticut or Massachusetts license is okay for most of it. Fishing closes here at the end of February, as it does in many other lakes to accommodate trout stocking.

What's unusual about Colebrook ... no, peculiar in fact... is that the primary fish sought after is not much bigger than bait. In fact, it is bait in many a body of water, because the target here is smelt each winter!

Smelt, those wonderfully tasty little shiny green critters that, properly cooked, can be eaten, bones and all. So, smelt are here, and quite a few smallmouth bass, yellow perch, and trout.

The lake covers 700 acres and that gives the smelt lots of places to hide from the other three occupants.

5,210 trout were stocked in one year, with 80% of them rainbows. The rest were brook and brown trout.

TIP: Smallies like to eat alewife herring when they can catch one, but the law here denies an angler the use of alewives, for good reason. They compete with the smelt for plankton as food so in order to allow smelt to eat and propagate, please don't break the law and bring any kind of herring or shad to this lake!

Another fish found in Colebrook is the red-eyed rock bass. In 1989 Ernie Gonsalves established the state record with his 1.3 pound specimen.

42 — COVENTRY LAKE

Also called Waumgumbaug, with a name like that, it's small wonder that the lake is usually referred to as the name of the town that it is in.

Coventry is a 377.5 acre impoundment, and can be found by traveling south off Route 31 on the first blacktop road west of South Coventry Access area which is about ¾ of a mile from Route 30, Southwest of the dam. If you are coming from town, then head north on 31. The fee boat ramp is in the southeast corner of the lake.

One of the most sought after fish in this lake is what some anglers call a "lowly" fish, the yellow perch. I am not among those folks because, when I want to take a few fish home for a meal, yellow perch are numero uno on my "best" list, period. They are not great fighters, but for certain, are wonderful on the dinner plate.

TIP: The center of the lake drops down to 36 feet and if you are after perch in late November, try here. I'll bet you will catch several pre-spawn fish right at the bottom.

Largemouth and smallmouth bass inhabit the lake, as do some slab sized bluegill sunfish and stocked trout.

You cannot use any herring or shad as bait. Another regulation says that the lake is closed from the last day in February until Opening Day of the trout season.

A very intelligent rule says that you cannot operate a boat and have any alcoholic beverage on board at the same time.

At night, you may not go faster than 6 mph. Ditto from noon to 4 p.m. from 5/15 to 9/15, and also from noon to 2 p.m. on July 4th. Again, each of these safety rules makes sense to me. Speeders, with or without somebody standing on sticks, can crank up to 40 mph at other times.

1,830 brown trout were stocked in the 99/00 year, and the

records I read showed none the prior season, but 2,630 went in the year before that. Chances are that in most years, an adequate number of trout will go in to please the spring cabin fever crowd. I also found out that in the fall of 2000, lots of trout were caught so the lake may very well get a fall stocking from time to time too.

When the ice is safe, an ice-fishing derby takes place at nearby Patriot's Park. Although bass come up through the holes, the target is, again, big yellow perch! Some pickerel have been taken that way too, according to an ice fishing report from the state at the start of 2001. Go with standard tip-ups and shiners, but since perch are the featured performer, use medium sized ones, not jumbos.

Early morning bass action is very good in the summer, but perch will whack a small grub at any time of the day.

Waumbgumbaug/Coventry, a fine lake for perch and bass.

43 — CRYSTAL LAKE

There's a Crystal Lake in Middletown, but this one is at Ellington/Stafford, 30+ miles away to the northeast, pretty close to the Massachusetts line.

To find this "Trophy Trout" lake, take 140 east from Ellington and turn left (north) on 30 and halfway up its western side is where you will find the boat ramp.

Called a "Trophy Trout" lake, during Open Season, the slot length is from 12 to 16 inches, and five legal fish can go home, but not more than one of 16 inches or better.

In the early part of the season, most good fishermen take a gang of trout by trolling. Catches of 20 or more per angler are quite common as the fish feed aggressively.

Over a very recent two-year period of stocking, the DEP put an incredible 31,900 trout in the lake, with more brown than rainbows stocked.

TIP: Try "jerk-trolling" at cold times. While you may want to drag a spoon on one stick, hold another rod with little or no weight at all, and a tandem of two large streamers. As the boat moves forward, jerk the rod forward and as the flies starts to slowly flutter back, many a trout will attack.

As the water temperature starts to rise, the trout head deeper, with 15 feet a good depth to troll at mid-spring, but head down to 20 or more around July 4th yearly.

Largemouth and smallmouth bass are in Crystal, with a good number of pickerel, yellow perch, bluegills and crappie.

The largemouth bass action is usually very good near shore on topwater stuff early or late in the day in the summer.

At times though, you may find them hiding in 15 foot deep wood right in the middle of the day.

Rainbow trout often will go after a mealworm at night, and if you pop one up with a miniature marshmallow, this will add to your chances. Brownies prefer a shiner or fathead though.

Take your kid here for a shot at bluegills, and remember, they may also catch some crappie, perch, etc.

The lake is not all that big, only 200 acres, but it holds 48 feet in the middle. Special speed rules apply here so to be certain that you are up-to-date on them, read up.

44 — EAST TWIN LAKE

Get ready for a big headache now, because some folks call this site "Twin Lakes," and in fact, there are two separate bodies of water, with "West Twin Lake" hooked on at the southwest end of East Twin. (And, oh yes, to confuse you further, East Twin is known as Washining and West is often called Washinee.) Some old folk lore involves two Indian Princesses or something, but honest, I don't care, so let's talk about the fishing, and in particular, at the far bigger East Twin, which covers 550+ acres.

Kokanee salmon were stocked into East Twin in sizable numbers but someone put some alewife herring in (herring and shad cannot be brought here) years ago and they have spread out, competing with the kokanee for one of their main food supplies, plankton. So while kokanee have disappeared, let's discuss what else is available.

First, to reach it. Turn north on a blacktop road off Route 44, one mile west of the Housatonic River. Twin Lakes Road runs around its eastern shore.

*Gary T. with the fine 4.11-pound chain pickerel he caught
at E. Twin Lake. (Photo courtesy of O'Hara's Landing.)*

The boat ramp charges a fee. And if you don't have your own rig,
you may want to consider renting one from O'Hara's Landing.
(860-824-7583).

A whole pile of rules pertain to the lake, including (who cares)
numbers of water skiers allowed per boat, speed limits, range away
from other boaters, etc. Most important though is that you could
only keep one brown trout among a five trout limit in 2001. And
that brownie had to be at least 20 inches long. 20,000 trout are
commonly stocked into the lake yearly. About half are browns.
Samuel Wright broke the previous state record with his brownie in
1986. It weighed 16.14 pounds.

Besides trout, the primary target is a largemouth bass. In one
early day in 2000, a 5.5 largemouth bass was caught and put back
along with a less common smallie, at a full 4 pounds. Paul Liphardt

checked in with a 5.2 brownie a week or so later. As spring moves forward, the holdover brownies get football shaped and while trolling is probably best, live bait will work well.

TIP: Try to have a good, accurate fishfinder on board. Set up in deep water, on a slope, with two anchors. Stick one in and then the other, hoping to have one anchor in at a depth of at least five feet more or less than the other. And now get serious with the fishfinder. Look for readings and drop a weighted shiner down to just a bit higher than where you see marks. The readings are at the thermo-cline, and since trout generally feed upwards, they will see the bait just above them and attack (we hope) with vigor!

Some of the best bluegill sunnie action is found in East Twin Lake so here again, bring a child or two with you.

If you would like to try for an assortment of fish, you might troll first for trout, and then fish the shallow weed beds for large bluegills and then give a shot at the rocky shoreline areas for big yellow perch.

Pickerel are also in East Twin, as are bullheads and some crappie.

45 — GARDNER LAKE

Covering 487 acres, this lake can be found at the edge of three towns: Salem to the west, Montville over east, and Bozrah to the north. It's about six miles west by southwest of Norwich, and from that city, take Route 2 west onto 354 south, and now east in Salem just north of Route 82. An alternate would be Exit 23 off Route 2 to 163 south and then west on 82. Extensive access is provided at the lake for persons with disabilities.

Gardner Lake contains a few species of fish that are not commonly found in Connecticut. First is the white catfish, and next comes one of, if not the best tasting fish available anywhere, walleye.

You can tell the basic difference between a white catfish by its color first, and then by the fact that it's tail has a slight fork to it, not as deep as in a channel cat, but also different from the conventional straight tail of a bullhead. Of course another difference is that

Project Leader Jerry Leonard shows off a Connecticut walleye
from Gardner Lake in Salem.

they can be far, far heavier! A monster white was caught in the
Connecticut River in 1999 that weighed 12.12 pounds!

TIP: If you are after big catfish, just about the best bait of all is a
gob of raw chicken liver. Just remember to bring a towel with you
because your hands will get messy otherwise, big time. Chicken liver
casts off pretty easily though, so you will need to "feather" your cast.

Walleye are the main target at Gardner to lots of anglers, and
since many are taken at dark times, you need to know that a speed
limit is in place that requires you to stay at or under 6 mph from
sunset to 8 a.m.

Two fish that rank up there in both popularity and numbers are
chain pickerel and smallmouth bass. Largemouth bass, brown

bullhead, crappie, sunfish, yellow perch and trout round out the large number of inhabitants in this lake.

It's not very deep, with 18 feet as the most commonly found depth, but you can find a small area of 30-42 feet ahead of you to the right of the boat ramp. This ramp is a good one and there is room for as many as 50 cars with trailers. The launch is down at the south end.

Brown and rainbow trout, plus some brookies are stocked along with walleye. A recent year saw 8,440 trout put in with most of them rainbows, as well as another 7,300 'eyes.

The lake gets some of its water from Whittle and Sucker Brooks and drains into Gardner Brook to the north.

The north shore is undeveloped, and along its northeast end you will find Hopemead State Park. Much of the rest of the area around the lake is highly developed.

Walleye have already reached two feet in length here and since they grow lots bigger, expect to find some soon that reach or exceed 7+ pounds or more. Big yellow perch are caught as well, up to 2 pounds. Try the walleye on night crawlers jigged just off bottom in dark times and for the best perch catches by day, go with a 1-2 inch grub.

A huge supply of bass is here too, with more bronzebacks than bucketmouths. At least ten different critters may be caught in a given day, so get ready for a fun outing.

46 — GREEN FALLS RESERVOIR/POND

Shh! Car-topped boats are the only ones that can get in at the ramp, which is up along its northwest corner. If you need a motor here it can only be electric. There is a fee charged for use of the ramp on weekends and holidays.

The lake isn't even identified by name in my copy of the Atlas, but it is found off Route 138 in Voluntown, off the access road south to Green Falls State Park. Signs will lead you to the launch site.

Besides fishing, this is a family spot, with no alcohol allowed, and it offers camping, swimming, hiking and picnicking too.

Trout are stocked in Green Falls Reservoir, with half of the

1200+ brook and the other brown trout.

TIP: For stocked trout, fishing from shore, use a baby night crawler and Power Bait sandwich. First stick the point of your #6 bait holder hook into the head of the worm, running the shank completely through the head, and then add your flotation bait (Power), and now stick the worm again through its body, half-way down. The trout can go after the smell (Power) or the wiggle (worm). It works.

We will not talk much in the book about small bodies of water, but this one seems to be a good one to discuss anyway. It only covers 49 acres and drops down to 27 feet at its deepest section down at the south side of the pond.

The lake has lots of sunfish too, along with largemouth bass and bullhead.

So if you want quiet, but somewhere to take the family to, try Green Falls Reservoir, but it closes on 10/31 yearly.

47 — HATCH POND

Another small but good lake is Hatch Pond. It is 61 acres in size and is in Kent. Another car-topper lake, you may use a small kicker here, but speed limits are restricted to 8 mph. And on so small a pond, who needs more anyway?

Access is Route 341, and south on South Kent Road, then west on Bulls Bridge Road, The launch is 200 feet to the right, and upwards of 15 vehicles can park near it.

Much of the pond is shallow, and gets kind of weedy, so your best bet would be to either fish early in the year before the green grows too high, or learn to use a weedless lure quickly.

TIP: Crappie are the most popular occupant, and since early spring means calico, find some overhanging wood. A long and light cane pole may be all you need. Tie on a length of 10 pound test mono that is a bit longer than the bamboo to the skinny end, add a little float, a very small split shot, and a size 10 light wire hook. Your best bait would be a fathead minnow, head hooked. Calico/crappie, can be lots of fun this way, and make a dandy meal too.

Yellow perch are in Hatch in good numbers, and other players are bullhead, pickerel and largemouth bass. If you are after the bass and pickerel once it warms up, make sure your spinner bait is as weedless as it can get. An alternate would be to throw topwater weedless stuff.

Right close by to the west are first Glasgo and then Pauchaug Ponds, also found in the book.

48 — HAYWARD LAKE
(a/k/a SHAW LAKE)

Not considered a lake that holds many, white perch popped up in good numbers in the reported catches to the state mid-summer in 2000!

Hayward is a pretty good-sized lake, covering nearly 190 acres, and is another electric-only spot. While it has a good ramp way up on its northeast tip, weeds can be a problem when you put the boat in.

Access is by taking Route 11, exit 6, E. Haddam, and west on Lake Hayward Road, approximately 1½ miles south of Colchester. It's another of those lakes that starts with the word Lake but remember, going by alphabet, this book always starts with the proper name word first.

Nine hundred or so trout go in annually, mostly rainbows.

I remember two anglers lecturing me many years ago along the shoreline of the Delaware River about their favorite "game fish." While these fish do fight aggressively, especially at the start of their battle, you can have each and every one that can be found in this lake, and you don't even have to say thank you to me! I am talking about one of Hayward's primary tenants, the American eel.

TIP: Just remember to bring a few towels with you if you go after them. One throwaway model for holding a squiggler, and the other for your hands themselves.

In the summer, a good number of fat bluegills can be caught by throwing a popper into shaded shorelines. But make sure your drag is not cranked down tightly because one of the many pickerel or largemouth bass that are here might beat the sunnie to the gurgling lure.

Black crappie are in Hayward, with many a yellow perch and

bullhead as well. In fact, John D. Rathburn caught a 3 pound brown bullhead in 1969 and it set the state record. So for variety, try Lake Hayward/Shaw Lake. It has many a fish to please just about everyone.

49 — HIGHLAND LAKE

Here's another lake in the state that had some kokanee salmon, but as with some other lakes, they are gone! That's because the kokanee could not compete with the alewives that a fool brought to the lake one day for their main food source, plankton. A state record was established in 1976 by David Randolph when he caught his 2¾-pounder, but don't count on breaking the record at Highland.

So while you won't catch any kokanee, you can still have a fine day on Highland Lake. It is in Winchester, and has special rules that apply for trout. During the open season the slot lengths are from 12-16 inches and five is the maximum number you may keep, with only one at or longer than 16 inches.

You can reach this 444-acre lake from Route 44/183 in Winsted, then west on Lake Street at the Route 263 junction. Now bear right onto Boyd St., and turn left onto Woodland Ave, then a right at the end of that road to the launch on the left where nearly 50 vehicles may park. The fee ramp is at the northern tip of the lake and a variety of speed and boat size rules apply, so — read the rulebook!

Even though the lake has depths ranging down to nearly 60 feet, it ices over hard in very cold winters, and offers superb yellow perch action along with largemouth bass at such times. Rainbow and brown trout come through the ice too often.

TIP: And we are not kidding here! Do not EVER be the first one on the ice. Make sure that you see at least one or two big anglers standing out there before you venture forward. This one should not need any explanation. And please leave the squashed fermented dark berry juice at home.

I think someone stole a bay or something. The north end is called First Bay and the southern section is referred to as Third Bay in the Atlas. I guess you can say that the middle is "Second," but it is not shown thusly.

Huge numbers of trout are stocked each year, upwards of 20,000+, with less than half 'bows and the rest browns.

Remember that they are trying to keep this a "Trophy" trout lake so don't forget that these rules apply. The lake is closed from 4/1 to Opening Day.

As you head down south from the ramp, you will reach 50+ feet depths a little less than halfway towards the other end. At this site, you may have your best shot at holdover trout because once the water warms up, they go deep. So if trout are your target in the summer, try to double-anchor over deep water on a weekday when the fast boats are not out yet. Look on your fish finder before starting to fish, and then drop your shiner down to just above the level you have readings at. If you are good at rigging a "slider float" ("slip-bobber"), try reaching them that way. Chances are good that out in the deep, nearly everything you read will be a trout.

Fine fishing can be found right near the boat ramp from shore early or late in the season.

We told you above that largemouth bass are taken through the ice. Well, forgetting trout, largemouth's are the number one sought after AND caught fish in the lake, year 'round. Fish them above structure early or late in the day during the summer. Some smallies are also in Highland with crappie and the ever-present sunfish as well.

50 — LAKE LILLINONAH (POND BROOK)

Among the very best rivers in the entire eastern coast is the Housatonic, and we went into great detail about it in the river part of this book. The Housatonic dumps into Lake Lillinonah in Bridgewater to the north. The lake stops to the south at Sheraug Dam, Newtown, where the river starts again. Lake Zoar, to also be discussed later, does the same thing, starting at a lower hunk of the Housatonic and stopping further south, as you will see.

The ramp to the north end as well as the one below both charge a fee, and all the basic laws that apply to the Housatonic are applicable at this very large 1,900-acre impoundment. Both parking areas are extensive.

The north area is reached on the east side of route 133, about nine miles south of New Milford. The ramp at its southern end can be found, also off Route 133, turning south onto Obtuse Rock Road just before the bridge in Brookfield. Then the road becomes Dinglebrook Lane in Newtown. The next left after Hanover Road will get you to the launch site.

Lillinonah is a site for serious tournament bass anglers to visit. Small and largemouth bass are just about everywhere, in substantial number and considerable size.

While you may find some trout here, again, bass rule! White perch are very common, as are the fish that make our visitors from Great Britain nuts... carp. Calling themselves "Carpers," my fellow members of Carp Anglers Group are indeed enthralled by the carp numbers in Lillinonah.

The balance of the population includes northern pike (a record was set in this lake back in 1980 by Joseph Nett when he caught a 29-pounder), black crappie aplenty, sunnies and yellow perch. Three bewhiskered citizens are white catfish, yellow bullhead and brown bullhead.

Bass anglers, of course, swear by the use of artificials.

TIP: A Rat-L-Trap works well in the spring at 6-8 feet down for largemouths.

For smallies, some guys love to throw lures around the bridge abutments and docks (providing they can get down to a 10 foot deep level with their lure where the fish are).

Try a dark jig around the wood too for crappie, and of course live bait is often the best way to go. Be it a large shiner for largemouths, a crayfish for smallies, or a fathead for perch and crappie, just remember to cut your leader close to the mouth of the fish if you cannot easily remove the hook. Nearly all will survive to eat again!

51 — LONG POND

I fished this well-named lake several times with my grandchildren, Rebecca and Joseph, and our target was trout. We caught quite a few, with a ton of sunnies outracing the trout for bait as the cold spring water started to warm up. So remember, for trout, start a day or two after Opening Day and you may not get so many sunfish.

The pond is in No. Stonington, and is a little less that 100 acres in size. Turn south on Lantern Hill Road off of Route 214 to reach the ramp at its northern end. Please watch your speed because there are some nasty turns.

TIP: For put 'n take trout, throw five or ten kernels of corn out at a time to "sweeten" the spot. Don't chuck out large doses because just stocked fish have no idea when to stop eating, and if they ingest enough corn, they may have difficulty digesting them (as we do).

There are some very pretty looking rocky areas that can be found here, but even though such water is where you are certain a pile of smallmouth bass can be found, it is not the case. Instead, largemouths are the predominant member of the bass family, unless you want to count their paper-thin mouthed country cousins, calico bass. A good number of black crappie come out of Long Pond.

I remember talking to an angler who was returning to the boat ramp a few years ago and asking him what he had caught. His reply, with a smile, was "Pickerel, lots!"

Yellow perch make up the rest of the fish found at this relatively quiet lake, quiet, even though it is pretty close to civilization.

You can use a gasoline engine, but the speed limit is 5 mph, and the parking can handle 30-40 cars. Standing room for shore fishing is good and close to your car.

Amy Renaldi caught a 6 pound largemouth here in May of 2000, but again, trout are one of the main targets. Nearly 9000 were stocked in the 99/00 season alone!

The lake is deep, by Connecticut standards, with a quick drop-off very close to the ramp. Here you first reach 36 feet and then as deep as 66 feet of water. Target your trout down 20-30 feet in this area as the waters warm up.

Most of the lake is far less deep, with 6-12 feet areas commonly found, and here will be your crappie, pickerel, and bass, as well as the smaller fish discussed.

52 — MANSFIELD HOLLOW RESERVOIR
(a/k/a NAUBESATUCK LAKE)

About average size for the locations in this book, Mansfield Hollow is far from average as to what it contains. The reservoir holds some of the largest numbers and sizes of northern pike found in all the state! To sweeten the population, Connecticut adds new fish yearly, with 2,691 fingerlings stocked in 1999-2000.

The boat ramp is on the western side of the lake, halfway down it shoreline, and may be reached by taking Route 195 north out of Willimantic. After you pass Willimantic Reservoir on the right, but before you get to Mansfield Center, turn east for a few miles to the ramp. It's tricky to find the right road so check at a gas station to be sure. The launch is owned by the Army Corp. of Engineers and is free, but please note that the lake is part of a State Park and therefore is a no-alcohol site.

Yellow perch are in the lake in goodly numbers, with a very large population of largemouth bass. Other panfish in here include hand-sized bluegills and crappie.

TIP: If your target specimen is pike, forget the wire! My own personal experience in catching hundreds of pike involves a careful comparison of fishing with and without wire leaders. It is true that you will get cut off from time to time otherwise, but I feel strongly that you will get more than double the hits with no wire!

Speed limits on the lake are restricted to 8 mph. And since you don't have anything on your boat that measures your speed, go slower rather than faster, just in case.

The north basin of the lake is a very good area to find northern pike. Some logs to 20 pounds have been taken there on large crankbaits. This area is particularly good in the end of the spring. And largemouth bass turn on all at the same time right near them.

Try the west side of the lake for bluegills, and don't be surprised if you catch one that goes as much as a pound.

Chain pickerel and trout were commonly found some years ago, but don't count on catching many of either any longer. Concentrate more on pike, bucketmouth, yellow perch, crappie and sunfish. There's plenty of each.

Mansfield Hollow is a very good lake for ice fishing. The launch area is a narrow funnel, with a bottleneck that holds several sheltered sections. As with most ice fishing, try coves before anything else, because they get good, safe ice first. Just remember the Gone Fishin' safety axiom... don't be the first one out there.

53 — MASHAPAUG LAKE/POND

The lake is in Union, right up at the top of the state, just before the border with Massachusetts. More than 10,000 trout are stocked annually, with a handful of brookies included in the heavy rainbow and good number of browns put in.

You can find the lake in Bigelow Hollow State Park, off Route 171. If you are taking the section of 171 that travels westerly, you will first hit Bigelow Pond, another little lake that holds trout. It is electric only. Mashapaug itself has a 10 mph speed limit, and the ramp charges a fee. Handicap access can be found here too!

The launch site is in the southern tip of the lake.

Besides trout, featured occupants include both small and largemouth bass; in fact, you may find more smallies than largemouths in your day's catch. Pickerel and yellow perch, plus sunfish are the other primary inhabitants.

Some wonderful depth changes can be found, with humps and bumps galore. About halfway up the lake you will reach its maximum, 42 feet, but very quickly after putting the boat in you will reach 30-foot levels. 12 foot chunks are commonly found and if you have a good depth finder, read it until you go from deeper up to this level and then try for your bass, mid-day.

Spring and fall stockings of trout create excellent fishing, but if bass are your target, work those humps.

TIP: If you can hold in position, throw a sinker free crawfish to more shallow water and wait. As it settles down towards bottom, a bronzeback will often head it off.

Trolling 20-foot levels produces too, for all three fish, largemouth, smallmouth, and trout. Try a small jointed stick bait in yellow perch finish.

Chain pickerel are usually taken here near shore, but you never know when they might venture out into the middle. I caught a 22-incher in July of 2001 in the middle of a lake in New Jersey, while double-anchored over 125 feet of water. The fish took a dead alewife herring held 24 feet below the surface under a slider float. Natural? No, but it worked.

There's not too much parking at Mashapaug, maybe room for 10-15 vehicles so in order to assure yourself of a place to park, try fishing a weekday.

54 — MOHAWK POND

This is just about the smallest piece of freshwater we will discuss, but lots of people feel that, for its 16 acre size, it should be in the "75 Best," so here goes:

Mohawk Pond is bounded by Cornwall and Goshen in Litchfield County. It's not much more than an unnamed blue dot of water on my DeLorme Atlas, with a boat shown therein. Take Route 4 to Great Hollow Road south and then east on Great Hill Road to the launch ramp.

Because it is modest in size, no motors may be used here, but the ramp itself is paved and trailed boats can be put in as well as car-toppers. About 10 vehicles can be parked.

Early in the year, trout are the fish that most anglers target. As with most trout stocked lakes, the waters are closed from the end of February to Opening Day so that the temptation to catch (and even to release) just stocked trout can be eliminated from your mind. Give 'em a chance to get acclimated to the lake before fishing. It is also the law, of course.

Considering its rather modest size, it gets lots of trout! 3,080 in all were stocked one recent year. 850 were brookies, only 300 were browns, and the rest were rainbow.

TIP: Want to know the difference between the three? Well, clearly, anyone can identify a rainbow because it has that reddish-purple marking from head to tail, and is more silvery. The brookie is distinguished from a brown by looking at its bottom fins. They have a white stripe on their edge.

In addition to "adult" (9-12 inch) trout, the state sweetens the water some years with little troutalettes, 6-8 inchers. I am not about to lecture you here, but if you are not out to take everything home, try to be a sport. Use a small, barbless hook. But if the fish swallows it, clip your line without removing it from the water and watch it swim away with a happy face. Most will survive to eat again another day if you do this.

27 feet of water can be found in the middle of the little lake, and while largemouth bass are mostly caught near shore, some nice sized fish can be nailed on live bait out in its deeper sections.

The lake ices over well and at this time, yellow perch reign supreme. Try a little ice jig, tipped with a mousee or wax worm for good results. Some fall-stocked trout too will sweeten your catch at times.

55 — MOODUS RESERVOIR

Moodus is a "Bass Management" lake, with special rules. In order to assure that they grow to trophy size, you cannot keep one unless it is at least 15 inches long.

There are two separate parts to Moodus Reservoir, with a ramp at the northeast tip of the top section, and another along the northwest section of the bottom part. And to confuse you further, Bashan Lake, another of our "75 Best," is just a short distance to the south of it.

Moodus is dissected by E. Haddam Colchester Turnpike. It holds 451 acres overall. The upper part is reached two miles east of Moodus off Route 149. Route 151 to E. Haddam Colchester Turnpike is a good way to find the lower end.

Both halves have the same rules regarding bass sizes, as well as speed limits. You can get up to 35 mph during the day, but from 9 p.m. to 8 a.m. the limit is 8 mph

This is very shallow water, but still it allows water skiing. That conjures up an image of boats hitting bottom with folks flying through the air, rocket-like, but I guess it doesn't happen. No disrespect intended, but the less water skiers the better for me anyway.

Moodus gets heavy weeds as its shallow water warms up so if

you are not into weedless lure casting, you may want to only fish it early or late in the year. The north lake gets even more weeded than the southern section.

TIP: When fishing weeds, try a dark grape/purple weedless six-inch plastic worm. Use a small sinker and after you hit the water, stop, dead. Wait at least ten seconds before starting a very slow retrieve. When you feel weight, slam hard. It may be that you got hung up, but you also might have gotten inhaled by a big bucket-mouth.

The lake has lots of pickerel, crappie, yellow perch and sunfish too, as well as some brown bullhead.

Some folks feel that, even though the top part has more weeds, it produces more quality bass. While bass are the main attraction, try throwing a weedless grub and jigging it back to the boat. A half-dozen yellow perch could sure make a fine meal and you have a good opportunity of doing just that here.

56 — MOUNT TOM POND

Another electric only lake, 61.5 acres in size, you really don't need gas, but please realize that you must check for a wind/weather report before heading out. Car-toppers can launch down at the southern tip but it is a long way back from the upper end in a strong breeze from the south.

The pond is off of Route 202, and the closest little town is Woodville. It is in Mt. Tom State Park, Litchfield Co.

A large number of rainbow trout go in yearly. More than 4,000 are typical, with another handful of brook and brown trout as well.

TIP: Some folks like to fish Mt. Tom at night for trout. Use something visible and smelly for rainbows. Try a butter worm popped up by a miniature marshmallow.

Rainbows do favor one kind of worm or another, but if brownies are what you are after, use a fathead minnow held a few feet below a bobber with no sinker at all. If you have access to them, saltwater killies are even better. They will head down naturally, with no lead to encumber them. And Mr. Brown Trout will be waiting with open mouth.

While 42 feet of water can be found in the middle, lots of folks fish here right from shore for top action. The lake is best fished early for trout and then as it warms up, target largemouth bass and yellow perch. Fall stockings of trout bring action from them again at that time.

The second most commonly found fish in Mt. Tom is the lowly but wonderful — for-kids sunfish. Black crappie are other favored tenants.

57 — NORTH FARMS RESERVOIR

Here's a good little pond with shallow water, where largemouth bass are the boss. They don't have much competition from other fish. The main other species are sunfish and brown bullhead, but chain pickerel are in the lake too to add spice and variety.

The lake is in Wallingford, just north off of Route 68, a mile or so west of I-91 at exit 15. The ramp is at its lower end and as many as 20 cars may park here.

Gasoline engines are permitted on its 62.5 acres, but you may not exceed 8 mph.

TIP: Bass have plenty of cover to hide in and for the biggest kind of fish, first catch a few little sunnies. Keep them alive and live-line one on a size 4 Aberdeen style hook. The bait will stay alive and bass love to eat what is naturally found in the lake. A pickerel might also take hold of the sunfish.

Try hooking your bait in the traditional way, behind the dorsal fin. But to entice strikes from fish you may have to put the hook into the mouth and out an eyehole. Then cast and slowly retrieve. This often works best.

Stickbaits get hung often in the weeds, but before the green takes over, try reeling them in with a fast, jerky retrieve for some fine pre-spawning bass.

Not much more to add, other than the state says that water skiing isn't allowed. Since the speed limit is restricted to not more than 8 mph anyway, combined with this other rule, you can bet that such water lovers keep far away.

58 — PACHAUG POND

Griswold is where this lake is located, in New London County. It's about 10 miles northeast of Norwich. Handicap access is at the dam. A special parking and fishing area for those folks is right here.

This is a pretty big lake, 870 acres overall, and to reach its ramp at the north end take Route 138. 40 vehicles can park at the ramp lot. Glasgo Lake is southeast of Pachaug off of Route 201 and you may want to try that spot too.

Pachaug has several islands that stick up out of the water. One is pretty close to the ramp and the other is well down at the other end.

TIP: *While there is no speed limit shown in the rule book, if you are out for an evening of fishing that reaches into black of night, please go slowly. A crash into the shore of an unseen island can be the last one you ever make.*

The Pachaug State Forest borders on the north shore, and the rest of the shoreline is privately owned so other than up at the top, boat fishing is all you can do.

16 feet is its deepest water, but most of the pond is only six to eight feet deep.

Pachaug received the largest number of pike that were stocked by Connecticut in 1999-2000, 3537 of them, and two years earlier it led the list also when 6,750 went into it.

Among the best action here is with pike and white perch, but I'm told that it is a "tremendous" lake for largemouths, even better than for the other two fish.

In addition to those three fish, pickerel, crappie, yellow perch, sunfish and bullhead are also caught at Pachaug.

A 6 pound largemouth bass was caught and released at the end of April in 2000 by a tournament bass angler. George Smith nailed yet another six-pounder, two months later.

Pike stocked only a few years ago (in 1999) were said to have reached 12-18 inches in length one year later. That is serious eating, folks.

The shoreline has lots of stickups, where bass are the main target. When ice out takes place though, count on crappie being

*Here's the kind of slab crappie that Ron Whiteley catches
in Southeast Connecticut on a fly.*

available just a foot or so below the oldest wood you can find
hanging over the water. "Blue-noses" (white perch) are caught in
large numbers off of any point of land you can find. They hang just
at the corners over shallow water.

59 — PATAGANSET (PATTAGANSETT) LAKE

The lake is off of Route 1, about a mile northwest of the juncture
of Route 1 and Route 161 in East Lyme. The launch is just a bit
north of Route 1, west of Route 161. Campgrounds are also right
near the boat ramp for those of you who like to spend some time
at a lake with or without family.

Some folks spell the lake with two "t's" at either end, and others
use a simple single "t" both times.

Speedboats, with or without water skiers, can only use the lake
between 6/15 and the first Sunday after Labor Day, and then only
between the hours of 11 a.m. and 6 p.m. At other times and dates,
the limit is enforced at 8 mph So, from we who don't like to get
knocked around in our little tin boats while fishing, Thank You,
Connecticut!

There's quite a bit of parking on site, for anglers and campers alike, but because it is in a populated area (and if you want to avoid the speedboats), fish until 6/15 or after the racers leave in September.

Since largemouth bass, a predominantly warm water fish, is the primary goal here, you certainly can and will catch them in the summer, but just fish before 11 a.m. or after 6 p.m. for the ultimate in personal creature comfort.

The water is only 3-6 feet deep for a while before you find deeper levels, and three quarters across the lake towards the other end it will reach 33-foot depths. Pataganset covers 123 acres.

Besides bass, it holds chain pickerel, black crappie, yellow perch, and sunfish. Some really big bluegills are in the lake.

TIP: For the ultimate in fly-rod pleasure, other than for the purists who only use the wand for trout with dry flies on wild water, get an assortment of little poppers. A black popper fished for an hour after sunlight or for the last hour of light is often the best way to go. Cast it to shore from your boat, or throw it out from shore. Just do what the lure name implies, "pop-it." The popping and gurgling will often entice the biggest nasty slab sunnies around. And if you are a saltwater devotee, one who really likes to catch porgies, just imagine what the scup would fight like on a fly rod. And then go catch a half-pound bluegill. It is a virtual duplicate!

This is another lake that, harumph, features the American eel. Good, you can have all of them. But for you lovers of such slimy specimens, I guess I had to tip you off.

In addition to the heavy population of eels, bass, and sunnies, the other main occupants are pickerel. Add crappie and yellow perch and that about rounds it all up.

The boat ramp is a good one, but remember that it gets heavy use in the summer and it is distinctly possible that the fast boats will not be ready to crank up and take off right away. You may find a boat sitting for quite a while as its occupants take a lifetime to take care of loading.

60 — PICKEREL LAKE

"Redmoon" (Troy Klauder) fishes this lake in Colchester, New London County. He told us that the main fish he goes after are largemouth bass, crappie and sunfish, but that pickerel also inhabit the 88.6 acre lake.

To reach the ramp up at its northern end, take Route 16 to the junction of Route 149. Turn south on 149 and then west for a mile and a half on well-named Pickerel Lake Road.

Like quite a few other lakes that Connecticut allows other users to visit, exactly like Pataganset which we just discussed, 8 mph is the maximum speed for much of the year. Check out Pataganset for exact other such rules.

I guess the main occupants once upon a time were pickerel, unless you want to stretch a point and say that the lake is kind of pickerel shaped, but that is really a stretch. Of course we have the Shark River in New Jersey, and while I have caught thousands of fish there, I sure have never seen a shark in that salt-water river.

TIP: If you are after a bass for a meal, remember that this is a slot-limit lake! The slot length is from 12-15 inches.

Summer is the best time, with the latter part of it even better than the early part. The water depth is only nine feet at most, with six feet being the most commonly found.

Several other fine waters among our "75 Best" that are nearby are Bashan Lake and Moodus Reservoir, just across the county line in Middlesex County.

Of course I don't have to tell you that you need a license to fish here, but because it has its own special speed and size limits, you can count on the man with the badge visiting often. So double-check that you are displaying it properly before traveling to Pickerel Pond.

61 — QUADDICK RESERVOIR

Largemouth bass and pickerel rule. Lots of them are here, and for lovers of both, read on to find out how to get there!

Located in Quaddick State Park, Thompson, you can find it four miles north of E. Putnam and Route 44. It's very close to the state line with Rhode Island, and not far from the Massachusetts border as well. The boat ramp is found on its upper eastern shore.

Another "Green Giant," northern pike, has been introduced to join with its cousins, pickerel, and as time goes on, the pike will grow to significant size. In fact, many of the northerns that were stocked in 1999 had already quadrupled in size a year later!

TIP: We told you this earlier, but it is worth repeating. When after pickerel or pike, forsake the wire leader. You will get cut off every five bites at most, but you will also get at least twice as many hits with no wire. Some of your fish will swallow the hook and still get to the boat because the line will swing around to the corner of their mouth where they have no teeth. In addition, besides those that are regularly hooked in the lip, you will notice that many of the fish are hooked from outside in — the hook will enter the mouth from the outside, and as such, your line cannot be chopped.

Over the two-year period from 1999 through 2000, the state stocked 6,815 northerns in the lake.

The approach to the gravel boat launch is narrow. As with many lakes, the parking may not accommodate you unless you either get there early (the gate is open at 8 a.m. and closes at sunset) or don't mind walking several hundred yards to the dock from where you had to park. A fee is charged on weekends and holidays, but that doesn't much cut down on the crowds at all.

The deepest water in the lake is very close to the ramp. It quickly drops down to 12 feet, and then progresses to 18 and then 21 — again, close to the launch and pretty much straight out.

In addition to the pickerel and pike, plus largemouth bass, yellow perch, bullheads, sunfish and black crappie round out the population.

Enjoy the lake, and if you catch a pike, try to practice "catch and release" so that they will grow to the monsters they are capable of becoming.

62 — QUONNIPAUG LAKE

Considered a "Trophy Trout" lake, this smallish 111.6-acre site is reached a bit east off of Route 77, above North Guilford. The ramp is up at its northernmost end, and has room for less than 10 vehicles.

For so relatively small a lake, it has two deep sections that hold 42 feet of water and a small hunk even ranges down to 48 feet one third of the way down its west side.

"Trophy" regulations include a creel limit of five trout, with a slot limit of 12-16 inches during the open season. Only one of your "keepers" may be 16 inches or better. The lake is closed after 3/31 to the third Saturday in April.

More browns are stocked than rainbows here, and that is probably because they grow faster. A typical year's growth for a brownie in a lake is a half-inch per month while the rainbow generally gains a quarter inch each month. A prior year's stocking included 7,000 trout with 5,000 of them browns.

TIP: If you are after quality browns in late Spring, and the lake is not crowded, try to position your boat over that narrow 48-foot hole. It runs parallel with the shore. Set two anchors, fore and aft, directly over the deep. If you have two or more anglers in the boat, you can each hang two lines down to where you read fish on your scope. If you were fishing on a drift or with a single anchor, this would be impossible. The more bait your boat can get down without tangling, the better, because you will simulate a small school of food to the passing trout.

A very significant number of largemouth are present at Quonnipaug. In addition, many a brown bullhead is caught from shore and you can also catch pickerel, yellow perch, sunnies, and the altogether nasty string of slime, the American eel.

Small in size, you don't need more than the 6 hp engine they allow you to use. And you may not use the engine at all between 9 p.m. and 6 a.m.

By the way, no one asked me but I really prefer the rule that restricts the size of your engine, rather than the more standard one that requires you to go no faster than ___ miles per hour. You really don't have a speedometer in your little aluminum boat, and that makes it difficult. I suppose this will require you to simply go slow, just in case, and on reflection, that's not a bad idea at all.

Of course with a horsepower restriction, that brings the thought power of some cheats up to a high level. Some clowns put a "6 hp" cover over their more powerful motor. A person with a badge though, upon seeing you move faster than six should carry you, is allowed to investigate and lift the cover. The serial number and at times, other markings, will give you away. Still more crooks will use two 6 hp engines, saying that their engines meet the law. I even saw a guy once with three engines on the boat in operation at the same time. Here again, get ready to pay the fine if you try it.

Ice fishing is not allowed at Quonnipaug Lake!

63 — RODGERS LAKE

Here's another fine lake to catch trout in, but the fish that is most sought after at Rodgers Lake is the largemouth bass, and the hot shots catch plenty of them.

You can reach the state owned boat launch site by taking Exit 70 from I95 onto Route 1 which travels first easterly and then up to the northeast for about 2½ miles to Laysville, then turning north on Grassy Hill Road. The lake is situated approximately 15 miles west of Groton.

The launch site can accommodate 20 vehicles with trailers. Remember though that a lot of people live close by, so you may be hard pressed to find space in a summer weekend.

Monster sized kickers are allowed, up to 135 horses. Those nasty "Personal watercrafts" can operate at times too. The Connecticut Boaters Guide (once again, get one, if you can), has regulations regarding when, where and how you may use a powerful motor, and the rules make sense. You do really need to study them though to make certain that you will be motoring within the regulations. I urge you to take a couple of aspirin a half-hour before reading the rules to avoid what otherwise is a guaranteed headache.

Remember that I said "Trophy Trout" lake? The 2001 Anglers Guide said that for the month of March, you could keep two trout only, and they have to be at least 16 inches long. That permits the state to stock earlier than 4/1 if they wish, and tells you that you

Jim Grabarek used a shiner at Rodgers Lake
for this fine largemouth bass specimen.

must release any little guys that you catch during March. Between 4/1 and Opening Day, though, the season is closed altogether.

A whopping 9,390 trout went in each year for 1999 and 2000. Most were brown trout. And for those who are after one of the few lakes in Connecticut that holds them, Rodgers also has received quite a few walleye until 2000. The state started adding 'eyes in 1993. Quick growers, they reach their 15-inch size limit in a hurry.

TIP: While the standard bag limit is five walleyes and they need only be 15 inches long, please try to stick to a smaller take home of larger fish. They are very good eating fish to be sure, but please try to conserve.

Rodgers is a very fine lake for ice fishing. For one thing, it gets quiet. No speed boats, no teenyboppers crashing by on their little noise machines. Just you and the fish!

Featuring yellow perch, pickerel, and walleye, the lake is a natural for hardwater anglers. And of course lots of trout come up through the ice as well as largemouth bass. Black crappie, catfish, sunfish, and, yuck-eels, are other fish that are caught with regularity here.

Rodgers holds nearly 265 acres and has an area halfway straight across from the ramp towards the west side that graduates down to 66 feet of water. This is where you will find some of the biggest trout suspended in the summer.

64 — LAKE SALTONSTALL

This is a "Bass Management" water, and you can actually see Lake Saltonstall as you drive north on I95 between exits 52 and 53 at East Haven. Most of it is well to the north of the road.

This is one of the few spots in the state that I will tell you about that cannot simply be walked out onto. You must first get a permit to fish here by calling the South Central Connecticut Regional Water Authority at 203-624-6671, ext. 339 (I hope they don't change it!!) The only boats you are allowed to use are available by renting from the Authority, and unless you bring your own battery and electric motor, it's arm power only.

Tip: The lake covers 410.8 acres and is one of the deepest lakes in the whole state. Therefore, please get a good, accurate weather report before venturing forth. You don't want to get caught in the open when a storm kicks up without a gasoline engine to bring you back to the barn.

The slot limits for bass are from 12-18 inches. The daily limit is six with not more than one being 18 inches or longer.

And with so much problems — permit, rental row-only, size limits, why Saltonstall? Because it is one of the really fine lakes in the state that holds a variety of game fish.

In addition to the bass, a couple thousand trout go in yearly, and it got 6,000 walleye in 1999/2000. They were not the only walleyes in the lake, however; Colorado resident Jim Geriski caught a 5-pounder in the spring of 2000.

Depths crash down severely once you move out from the dock. While you may not have a portable depth finder (if you do, it sure is a plus), you are in 60 feet quickly. Just a little across and to the

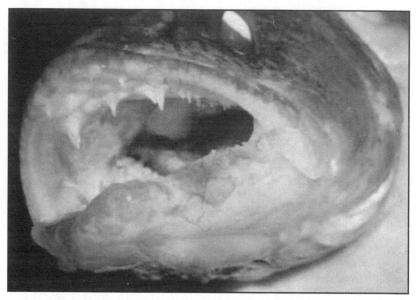

Not a pretty face, unless you caught it!
Here's the kind of walleye they get at Saltonstall.

right of the dock is as much as 100-foot depth.

A variety of fish join the walleye, bass and trout here. Lots and lots of bluegills and pumpkinseed are resident, making the lake quite kid-friendly. Black crappie, plus yellow and white perch add to the children's happy faces.

65 — SAUGATUCK RESERVOIR

Another water that requires a permit is Saugatuck. Call The Bridgeport Hydraulic Co. at 203-336-7788 to get one.

If you try to find the lake in your boater's guide, forget about it. Simply put, no boats are allowed! You are only allowed to fish the lake from its western shoreline. And you may not use any kind of herring or shad for bait.

So here we are again. Rules galore. Why include it? Because it is a very fine lake and if you do it right, you will really enjoy yourself. In addition, it has very fine handicap access as well.

Since the west side is where you can fish, get to it via Route 53

(Newtown Tpke) out of Weston. Take Godfrey Road EAST. Better yet would be to turn onto Valley Forge Road.

Four of the six main fish in the lake are considered "game fish," including trout, large and smallmouth bass, and walleye. Throw in crappie and sunfish and you know why we included the lake in the 75.

Besides fine fishing, some pretty scenery is here, and with no boats, the quiet is a wonderful plus.

In spite of its restrictions, the state is dedicated to making the lake a popular place. For example, it got over 12,000 trout, mostly browns, in two very recent years. The largest number of walleye stocked in a given year by the state went here too... 9,300 of them.

TIP: Make sure it is allowed first when you call Bridgeport Hydraulic for your permit, and if so, try night fishing. Walleye love to eat in the dark. Their huge eyes allow them to see clearly. Fish with a slider float and a 3-4 inch shiner as bait. Test the depth before setting your bobber stopper string. Ideally, you want the bait to settle down to a foot or less off bottom.

66 — SQUANTZ POND

Still more walleye! Connecticut wants its residents to enjoy catching walleye and as a result, they put some in here from time to time. But lots of other fish are in Squantz also.

Squantz is just to the west of Lake Candlewood and in fact, Route 39 north out of New Fairfield actually offers views of Squantz to the north and Candlewood to the south. The boat launch is situated in Squantz Pond State Park and 25 or more vehicles can park nearby.

While Candlewood allows speedboats, park rules at this 288-acre, 47 feet maximum depth lake allow no more powerful engines than 7½ horsepower.

In addition to walleye, trout are probably the most popular occupants. Largemouth bass are very common and both perch, white and yellow, reside as well. Some folks target a different fish and unless you have caught one, you might not understand. That critter is a carp!

TIP: For carp fishing, go simple. A forked stick from shore, propping up your seven-foot medium action spinning pole, is needed. Make sure your drag runs smooth. The rig is a half-ounce egg sinker stopped by a tightly clamped pinch on sinker a foot away from your size six bait holder hook. Add five or six kernels of canned corn and cast out. Put the rod down (be careful to not get the line stuck under the rod into the fork itself), and wait. Make sure your drag is wide open or get ready to wave goodbye to the rod, because a carp will often take off with the bait in a big hurry and take your rod and reel with her.

If you have never caught a 10+ pound carp, just wait. And once you learn how to catch them from a lake like Squantz, then you are ready for moving water, where they get even stronger fighting current all their lives. There is no freshwater fish, none at all, in the entire state, that can take so much line off your reel and stay away from you for as long a period of time as a carp can. And to those who laugh and say nay — when you break your line on your first run, remember, I told you so!

Walleye bite well here at night, as do carp, but if you have two lines out, one for carp and the other for walleye, count on the carp crossing the other line and tying knots in it during its fight.

The walleye hit in a variety of ways. Throwing or trolling crankbaits works all day at the end of April, but then as the water warms you really want to fish early or late only, unless it is a very dark day. A Rapala will do it, but nothing beats a live and frisky shiner. The Causeway area offers fine walleye action in the evening. Jigging worms is another style, as is trolling worm harness rigs.

Rainbow trout favor Power Bait in the spring, but trolling spoons for them 12-18 feet down is better for the bigger ones.

Squantz is a "Trophy Trout" lake, meaning that it is closed from the end of March until Opening Day. For the month of March you can fish; however, the creel limit is two and each much be at least 16 inches in length.

67 — TYLER LAKE/POND

For a lake that only covers 182 acres, the state wants it fished and puts 4,250 trout in, mostly rainbows. To reach Tyler, take Route 4 west from Torrington. Approximately 1½ miles west of the intersection with Route 63, turn right onto the SECOND Tyler Heights Road to the western side of the lake. The launch is on the right at the bottom of a hill. Note that you must back down from the street.

TIP: Not really a "fishing tip," but one that could save your sanity. Unless you have an SUV or are otherwise expert in backing down a hill, don't try this with any witnesses!

26.2 feet of water is found mid-pond, and the water quality is pretty good. The two main occupants are trout and yellow perch, but it also holds a bunch of crappie and bullhead. In addition, pickerel and sunnies reside herein.

The lake closes for trout stocking from the end of February until Opening Day, the third Saturday in April.

Good-sized brownies are caught here, in addition to the standard foot long browns and rainbows. Some come through the ice later and since the lake is a fine locale for the hardwater brigade, let's talk about that now

Standard tip-ups with shiners account for largemouth bass, pickerel and the occasional big brown, but you should always have a jig working through one of your holes.

Yellow perch are the main target. Use a chrome-plated jig that is tipped with a mousee. Rainbow trout will attack such a jig with great vigor and since so many are stocked you might catch one or two with your perch. And that jig might be stopped dead on the start of the lift by a far bigger fish, so keep your drag open just in case.

68 — UNCAS LAKE/POND
(a/k/a HOG POND)

Uncas is only a short ride away from Rogers Lake, one of our other "75 Best." Proximity to each other doesn't mean similarity in rules though. Rogers allows monster motors some of the time. Uncas doesn't allow any manner of engine at all. So if you don't know how to row well, get a friend to do it for you, or keep away.

Silence reigns supreme here at this small (69 acres) pond found in Nehantic State Forest, outside of Lyme.

Take Route 156 North in New London County, for 3.8 miles from I95, and turn east onto the access road into Nehantic State Forest. You will find room for 15 vehicles here. The ramp is well paved. Very little housing can be seen around the shoreline, adding to its scenic beauty.

As with many lakes, this one closes during the trout-stocking season from the end of February until the third Saturday in April. 2,730 were stocked in 1999/2000, with the largest majority rainbows.

Reports from the lake showed that fine catches of trout took place in both the spring and fall, and chances are anywhere from good to positive that all were recently stocked.

TIP: If you are after "catch and release" fun but want to catch your trout with bait, use a slightly bigger hook than you might otherwise try. Instead of a #10 use a #6, and squeeze down the barb. If you cannot remove the hook with ease, in spite of these attempts, cut your line and tie on a new one instead of trying to save a 10-cent hook. Nearly all will survive if you don't make them bleed.

Depths here reach down to 40 feet and the average is more than 22 feet, much deeper than normal in so small a pond.

Besides trout, and maybe more popular then them too, are the largemouth bass that roam the shoreline. As many eels maybe as both of them combined are here. Well, at least if you got the eels to hold still and measured them compared to the overall length of the trout and bass line, the eels will win, big time.

Chain pickerel, yellow perch and sunfish are the other fish caught in Uncas Lake. If you are so inclined, try to catch a little perch on a small piece of worm using a size 12 hook. Have a second rod rigged with an Aberdeen hook in size 4 attached. Head hook the perch through the upper lip and out one of its nose holes. Cast the fish out, with no sinker or float, and let it swim freely from shore or from your boat. You shouldn't be surprised if the perch suddenly moves away with vigor. That would mean that a bass or pickerel has it. Now get ready, and like the good old boys down south say, "Cross his eyes!"

69 — LAKE WARAMAUG

The bosses here are bass, large and smallmouth. Gaining momentum in popularity however, are chain pickerel. This rather large lake, 680.2 acres in size, offers several obstacles to the pleasure of some people, but they are far from severe and it is well worth a trip to get here and try out the action.

You can reach it by taking Route 45 north out of New Preston, then turning west on Lake Road and then get onto North Shore Road to the lake. You will be in Waramaug State Park.

Several obstacles exist, as noted. For one, unless you are a mountain man, you may need help getting your boat to the launch because it is a 150-foot carry to the water's edge. 15 or so vehicles can park here. There is a fee charged to enter, and because it is a State Park, Waramaug is of course a no-alcohol site. So if you have a small car-topper or canoe, it's fine, but realize that without power, you must carefully watch the weather.

The lake has a little chunk that drops down to nearly 40 feet, and near shore, its measurable depth is 26 feet, so you will be in pretty deep water not far from shore.

Besides fishing, visitors to the park can picnic, swim, and camp, (78 campsites available on a seasonal basis) and better than rustic restroom facilities are on site.

You will see some of Waramaug's eastern shore as you drive on 45 and then wrap around to the northwestern entrance.

Very significant numbers of both small and largemouth are in Waramaug. Largemouth specialists like to use Kelly scented worms in the summer. If you are not targeting one more than the other, and don't mind an occasional pickerel, the answer is live bait.

Alewife herring are native to the lake and if you can find a bait dealer that carries them, herring are #1 by far.

TIP: Since you certainly won't have a live bait well with pump in your little car-topper, in order to keep your herring alive, put them in a white rectangular container. A dark bucket will kill them quicker because its water will warm up faster. The larger bottom area of a rectangle will offer more area for the bait to swim in too than in a bucket of any color. And for sure, change the water often and add some loose ice. It will pay off!

While not shown in the State's stocking list, brown and rainbow trout are here in addition to the other fish that occupy it. Included too are crappie, yellow and white perch, plus bullhead and sunfish.

70 — WEST BRANCH RESERVOIR (HOGBACK)

The nearest town is Hartland, and very nearby its northern shore is Colebrook River Lake, separated from West Branch by the Colebrook River Lake Project. Get to West Branch (it is mostly in Litchfield but partially too in Hartford County), via Route 20. Go northwest on Hogback Road (thus the alias), then first left onto access road crossing the dam. The launch is owned and operated by MDC and upwards of 30 cars can park here. This is a car-top lake only.

Along the way up Hogback, you will pass parts of the Farmington River. More about this wonderful water can be found back in the river section.

While I couldn't find any specific details about trout stockings, the State reported good catches of trout in this 200-acre lake in the Spring of 2000.

What I can tell you for sure is that it is one of the few places in the state where you can catch smelt. And because it holds smelt, the use of any manner of herring or shad is strictly prohibited. Smelt eat plankton, as do herring, and the herring family members would compete with and probably overtake the smelt if they were allowed to be inhabitants.

To catch smelt, one way would be to use the same kind of rig that they use in Florida to catch live bait offshore. An example would be the Sabiki rig, which holds five or six very small dressed hooks with mylar on them. Put a half-ounce barrel sinker under the last hook and jig the whole deal up and down right after ice-out for optimum results. Don't take more than you need for a meal because they taste far better fresh than if you freeze extras.

Yellow perch and sunnies are other natural bait that the primary resident game fish seek, and that game fish is a smallmouth bass.

TIP: Since a little perch is shaped and slightly similar in coloration to a smelt, try row-trolling a jointed Rebel or Rapala stick bait for smallies. Pick a plug color that looks like these resident baitfish. If your lure comes roaring out of the water with a fish attached, not to worry, that's just a bronzeback showing its leaping skill.

By the way, 70,000 kokanee salmon fry were stocked here in 1999/2000, and if they take hold, they grow to mature size (12-16 inches) in three summers.

71 — WEST HILL POND

West Hill Pond, containing 238.8 acres, is another kokanee lake well known for its population of salmon. Drive to it from Winsted via Route 44 turning south on West Hill Lake Road and then the first right (Perkins Road) to the launch. 20+ cars can park here, but understand that the lake is drawn down after Labor Day so you will find less water in the fall then you found in the spring.

Horsepower restrictions exist from 6/15 to Labor Day, as do speed limits. The kicker cannot be more than a 7½, and 6 mph is the fastest allowed when it is dark out, with 15 mph during the day. Frankly, on so small a lake, I would rather the engine be restricted to the 7½ all year long. I guess that since most people who use the lake during the non-summer months are fishermen and therefore understanding of other anglers needs, it's okay though.

TIP: I caught a mess of kokanee out in Heron Lake, New Mexico this way early one morning, and I bet it works here too. Troll two lines from the stern, way up high, with small copper spoons. Put two kernels of corn on each hook, and add a few drops of trout attractant to each kernel before getting the lure in the water. After each fish caught or missed, re-do it again. New corn, new liquid smell, and over you go again. I bet you do well that way.

Huge numbers of trout are stocked annually too, and the lake is called a "Trophy Trout" lake. Most were browns (13,520 of them) and the rest (3,840 rainbows) went in during the 1999/2000 stocking year. Closed from 4/1 to Opening Day, for the month of March you can fish for and keep two if they are at least 16 inches in length.

Smallmouth bass are commonly found in the lake, and a lesser number of largemouths inhabit it. Chain pickerel are here as are yellow perch, sunnies, bullhead, and rock bass. Hopefully, with all that natural bait, the pickerel and bass will leave the little salmon alone to grow up.

It is extremely important that no one brings herring or shad in as bait because it is against the law! Remember, they eat plankton and compete with kokanee as a result. I've seen herring act like vacuum cleaners on the top of the water, sweeping up plankton galore. Please don't bring any for bait or else you will destroy this fine fishery.

Besides the trolling suggestion I gave you, try hanging mealies or grubs down from your boat at night. In the middle of spring you will find them in 15-18 feet of water but as it warms up, you may get your best results 35 feet down in 50 feet of water with the same kinds of bait. This deep water (52.5) can be found way down at the other end of the lake.

In the fall of 2000, kokanee that averaged 14 inches were collected here and brought to the Burlington Fish Hatchery to have their eggs removed and bred for 2001 stockings. Connecticut was thrilled then to find the largest number and size of such broodstock in quite a few years.

72 — WINCHESTER LAKE

Here's a 250-acre artificial lake site that features largemouth bass. For you bass lovers, it is a bit west of Winchester Center. From Route 263, travel on West Road to the boat launch on your right side.

The lake was formed by construction of an earthen and masonry dam on the headwaters of the East Branch of the Naugatuck River, and reaches down to a maximum depth of 17 feet. When they built the lake, a significant number of trees were not cleared during the filling. So if you know where you are going, the lake offers buried treasure galore, wood-wise, with tons of hiding places for bass to jump out of and pounce on unsuspecting passersby.

The whole lake shore is undeveloped, making it a fine site

indeed. The parking area holds 20 vehicles and the asphalt ramp itself is pretty good. Your boat cannot exceed 8 mph.

TIP: Bass anglers should try to find some of the many dead trees that stick up to just below the water line. Cast a four-inch dark plastic weedless worm here and bounce it along the wood. Bass will pounce from their hiding places.

A shiner on a float is one of the best ways to catch bass, of course, but with so many hang-ups, you had better be using very strong, abrasive free line to avoid being broken off in the wood.

Pickerel are in Winchester too, as are yellow perch and sunfish. A substantial stocking of northern pike fingerlings was done here in June of 2001 and, since they are fast growers, add that to the availability list for the future.

73 — WONONSCOPOMUC LAKE

Routes 44, 41 and 112 make a sandwich around the lake, just across the New York State line at Millerton. Lakeville is the closest town in Connecticut The boat launch is owned by the town of Salisbury and non-residents must pay $10 to put their boat in. Get here from Lakeville by heading 1,500 feet south of the junctions of 44 and 41 on Ethan Allen Street to the ramp.

In addition to the town having the right to charge a launch fee, they also own and will rent rowboats to you, so this facility is really ideal for anyone out for a fun day. You don't have to bring your own rig — you can rent one. I talked to Lisa at the boathouse who told me that they have a Fishing Derby for children at the start of the season each year.

Your own engine cannot be bigger than 10 hp, and fishing hours are from 6 a.m. to 8 p.m. The rental boats can be obtained from the boathouse but hours are a bit tricky.

Trophy sized brown trout inhabit Wononscopomuc (I think I'll call it "Wono" from now on).

The lake produces wonderful trolling for trout and as its water warms up, the fish are caught deeper and deeper. It has water as deep as 100 feet in the middle, but stick to less depth for your brownies. Try 12-18 feet down mid-spring, and then pull 20-25 feet below as summer begins. Later on, 30 feet down is better yet.

9,540 trout were stocked in each of two recent years with 7,000+ of them browns and the rest rainbow.

Unfortunately, its kokanee salmon population was cut back by the illegal introduction of alewife herring and just in case the state wants to try and start it up again, you may not use shad or herring for bait here for reasons we have already gone into at length.

TIP: If you are skilled in trolling, try using downriggers that hold your stickbaits down to the specific level you read fish at mid-lake. Those readings will probably be big brown trout. Since herring are in the lake, a Thin-Fin plug that is silver and purple will match the food fish.

The lake has a huge amount of changing depths from the livery out to a third of the way across to the other side. These slopes are the way to find trout because they really like to hang and feed here rather than over flat bottom.

While a lot of fish might still be feeding, the lake closes at the end of October so remember that this is not a year 'round place.

Add largemouth bass, pickerel, yellow perch, sunnies and catfish and that makes up the population of "Wono."

74 — WYASSUP LAKE

To get to Wyassup in North Stonington, New London County, take Route 2 and turn north onto Wyassup Lake Road. This lake will split to the left and right. Take the left fork! The ramp will be on your right and a handful of cars can park there. The lake is just a bit south of another of our waters, Billings Lake.

The lake is natural, but its level was raised when an earthen and masonry dam was built. It covers 95 acres and goes down to 24 feet of water halfway across the lake to the north.

Found here among only a few other waters in Connecticut are white catfish. Forgetting the tail split, the easy way to tell if you have a "white" is that if it is big, it is probably a white. Standard bullheads range to 3 pounds at best but a white catfish can be three or four times heavier. However, if it is little, the skin color will be lighter and less blotchy than a bullhead, and you can find a little fork in the tail if you look hard enough.

A handful of brookies plus some browns are stocked, but most of the 2,680 trout that went in recently were rainbows. The main bass is the smallmouth, and they are all joined by some large-mouths as well as pickerel, yellow perch and bullheads.

The lake closes for trout stocking between the end of February and the third Saturday in April.

Speed limits exist at this modestly sized pond (8 mph). But between 6/15 and the first Sunday after Labor Day, faster speeds with water skiing also can be done between 11 a.m. and 6 p.m. Therefore, we anglers are protected from the fast guys other than when it is probably too hot to go fishing anyway. Not bad at all, once you think about it.

TIP: If you want some of the pickerel found here and have been hiding in a cave since your birth, you may not know this — otherwise skip it — For those cave-dwellers, the best lure by far is a standard red and white Dare-Devl Spoon. Just throw it out and reel it back to the boat, pausing to let it fall periodically. This remains the top pickerel catching lure of all times!

75 — LAKE ZOAR

Last but not least in our list of the "Best" lakes is the second impoundment that was formed as part of the Housatonic River chain, Zoar. The northern lake is Lillinonah, discussed earlier. Zoar dumps back into the river as it continues southward towards the Sound.

To get to Zoar's boat ramp, you get teased a bit first. Take 84/6 northeast from Sandy Hook or Newtown, crossing directly over the water! Continue until exit 14 and then head south to Lakeside Road, and turn right on Lee Farm Drive to Scout Road and you will find the ramp at the end of this road. 60 vehicles can park here.

The lake covers 975 acres and has a vast number of quality pan fish. If you like action, try Zoar. All the regulations that are in place for the Housatonic apply here.

The boat launch is a good one, and the lake ices over well. When ice is on the lake, you will probably catch a mixed bag of black crappie, plus white and yellow perch.

TIP: If you can buy some live grass shrimp down the shore and keep them alive, they make the best kind of bait you can get hold of. A good second choice would be frozen grass shrimp, which still have the same smell and taste. And if ice is on top of the fish, they will be too cold to be particular anyway. Seriously, grass shrimp is great bait.

When the water is warm, fish a dark crappie jig 10 feet down around dock pilings and bridge abutments. Largemouth bass will hit your jig along with the crappie.

Topwater plugs worked over deep structure that you can find with your depth finder will do the trick for largemouths, but we haven't told you yet that the main bass is the smallmouth.

In addition to the many species already talked about, pickerel are in Zoar along with sunnies and catfish. If you are using a baby night crawler on bottom in the early spring after a rain and something takes hold like you never had on your line before and quickly breaks your line — chalk it off to your first experience with the beast I call "Mr. Man," carp! Plenty of them are here also.

HONORABLE MENTION
- **Black Pond — Meriden** — crappie, bluegill, bass & trout.
- **Glasgo Pond — Griswold** — bass, catfish, and panfish.
- **Park Pond — Winchester** — bass and perch, plus others.
- **Red Cedar Lake — Lebanon** — sunnies & perch at dam.

- AND... Worth mentioning and clearly, very commendable — the Gone Fishin' cap goes off to DEP for making three pieces of moving water and not less than 28 ponds in 24 towns available as "KIDS ONLY" waters! The list appears in the Anglers Guide each year. This really is a great idea!

See ya'on the water. *'Scuze me, gone fishin'.*